God, Christ and Us

God, Christ and Us

HERBERT MCCABE OP

Edited with an Introduction
by Brian Davies OP

continuum
LONDON • NEW YORK

Continuum
The Tower Building
11 York Road
London SE1 7NX

15 East 26th Street
New York
NY 10010

www.continuumbooks.com

First published 2003

British Library Cataloguing-in-Publication Data
A catalogue record for this book is available from the British Library.

ISBN 0-8264-7279-6

Typeset by BookEns Ltd.
Printed and bound by Antony Rowe Limited, Chippenham, Wilts.

Contents

Contents

Foreword

Christian philosophers do their job so that Christian (and other) people have a better chance of living free from idolatry – and so of praying with honesty and joy. There can be few Christian philosophers of the century past who have so fully exemplified this side of their vocation as did Herbert McCabe. Time after time, he will show how the classic shape of Christian talk about God punctures the silly or frightening or trivial models we create, so that we can become ourselves in the light and power of God's self. And at this level, there is small difference between the philosopher and the theologian; time after time, once more, Herbert McCabe shows us how the tradition of Christian talk that we associate with the giants of the early and mediaeval Church is the richest possible way to make sense of the Bible.

The result is more than just a book of sermons; it is an irresistibly direct, earthy, no-nonsense refresher course in Christian faith as such. Honest about practical and intellectual tangles, confident in a central mystery that both stimulates endless thought and eludes capture, grateful for grace these reflections are a brilliantly unusual guide to Christian and (in the fullest sense) Catholic reality, accessible to practically any reader. A precious legacy from a remarkable, exhausting and loveable man.

Rowan Williams
October 2003

Introduction

Herbert McCabe died in 2001. After his death, I edited a collection of his (largely) unpublished typescripts. This appeared under the title *God Still Matters* (London and New York, 2002). Like *God Matters* (London, 1987), which Herbert put together himself, it contained a small selection of sermons preached by him on various occasions. In 2002 I was hoping that Herbert's unpublished writings would yield material for an entire volume of sermons by him. And so they did. Hence the present collection.

McCabe was, and still is, highly regarded as the author of various essays on philosophy and theology. But, as befits a Dominican, a member of the Order of Preachers, he was also greatly appreciated for his sermons. And rightly so. For McCabe was an extraordinary preacher. As the distinguished philosopher Sir Anthony Kenny says in a review of *God Still Matters* (*Times Literary Supplement*, 20 December 2002): 'If you went to a sermon by Herbert, you knew you were in no danger of falling asleep.' That, of course, was partly because McCabe always preached in a lively and witty way (his style has been compared to that of G.K. Chesterton). But it was also because of what he actually had to say.

He was trained both as a philosopher and as a theologian. And, as is evident in what follows, this fact was notably reflected in his preaching. His sermons were never platitudinous or short on ideas. Instead, they were typically filled with questions, arguments and solid intellectual content, both philosophical and theological. The major theological influence on McCabe was, of course, the Bible. But he was also a devoted admirer of the thought of St Thomas Aquinas (1224/6–74), whose ideas saturated his public speaking (including his sermons) as well as his published writings. From the Bible, McCabe derived a notion of God as leading us to happiness through the work of grace and, especially, through the life and teachings of Jesus. From Aquinas, he derived a hatred of idolatry, a powerful sense of the incomprehensibility of God, and a recognition that we depend on God's gracious revelation of himself rather than what we can work out on the basis of our limited human understanding. From Aquinas, too, he learned to emphasize that our salvation is something achieved by the goodness of one like us. A presiding theme in many of his sermons is that we are saved because of the life of someone fully human.

Strongly convinced that preaching is an awesome task not to be engaged in lightly, McCabe never delivered sermons without a written text before him. This has made it relatively easy for me to edit the present volume. It also allows readers truly to be aware of what he had to say from the pulpit. In what follows, you will be pretty much reading what his listeners once heard. And you will, I hope, find that just as this was very much worth listening to then, it is also very much worth reading and reflecting on now.

Unfortunately, I am unable to determine where or when the following sermons were preached. And I should note that the titles under which they appear in this book are mostly my own. They are all previously unpublished, with the exception of 'Hope' (Chapter 2). This originated as a series of televised Advent sermons delivered in 1986 at Blackfriars, Oxford. It was originally published by the Catholic Truth Society in 1987. I am grateful to the Catholic Truth Society for permission to reprint it here.

Brian Davies OP

Chapter 1

Faith

The letter to the Hebrews tells us that 'Faith is the assurance of things hoped for, the conviction of things not seen' (Hebrews 11:1). This is a special way of looking at faith. For the author of Hebrews, faith has to do with what we do not *yet* see, what we hope for. It has to do with what is over the horizon. If you like, it is what lures us on to journey over the horizon to look at what we cannot yet see.

This approach to faith is, I think, very different from, for example, the notion of faith as a kind of test. There was a sort of an idea around when I was a child that God, or possibly the Church, proposed to us certain things that were difficult to believe or even to understand (that God is both three and one, for example), and we showed our loyalty (our faith) by accepting these propositions. If we were humble enough to accept things we couldn't understand, then we would eventually be rewarded for our devotion. The great enemy was always a thing called 'spiritual pride', which made you always want to understand everything.

That is one way of looking at faith. I don't think it's a very good way, but it's one way. And, when we are dealing with difficult and mysterious things, almost any way of seeing them is some help. But this way is very different from the way faith is looked at in Hebrews. Here, faith is all about trying to understand. It is about not being content to understand the things that are obvious, the things we can already see. It is about trying to understand what we do *not* yet see. It is about setting out on the journey to explore what we have not yet seen. We read: 'By faith Abraham obeyed when he was called to set out for a place that he was to receive as an inheritance; and he set out, not knowing where he was going' (Hebrews 11:8). Faith, for the author of Hebrews, is seen in terms of a journey, a movement. And not just a commuter's journey, a movement from one familiar spot to another. It is seen as a real journey, the kind of journey you make on a holiday, to see new places and to meet new people. It is a journey of exploration, an adventuring out.

This way of talking about faith is again different from another that you get in the Bible where we hear about the 'household of the faith' (Galatians 6:10). There, the faith is, so to speak, the badge of membership of the community. And we speak of those who are 'sealed with the seal of the faith', as we speak of 'preserving the faith', or 'preserving the deposit of faith'. Here 'the faith' is seen as a kind of treasure we have inherited (we talk of 'handing on the faith'). We are almost talking as though the faith were something we possessed. And this, too, is, of course, a valid way of talking. It brings out one aspect of what we mean by 'faith'. But, again, it is a very different approach from that of the letter to the Hebrews. For this text, the faith is not something we possess. It is all about what we do *not* possess. It is about what we hope for, and do not yet see.

For the author of Hebrews, the first image of faith is the journey of Abraham into the unknown, a journey simply based on a promise: not a planned journey, with all the arrangements made beforehand, but perhaps more like modern package tours, where you can't be sure the hotel has actually been built yet, where you are journeying toward the Promised Hotel. But then Hebrews makes things a little more complicated. In a sort of way, Abraham arrives at the Promised Land. But, even then, it is not something he possesses. 'By faith he stayed for a time in the land he had been promised, as in a foreign land,

2

living in tents, as did Isaac and Jacob, who were heirs with him of the same promise. For he looked forward to the city that has foundations, whose architect and builder is God' (Hebrews 11:9–10). The author of Hebrews is here remembering the Old Testament story according to which Abraham arrived as a wandering nomad in Canaan (the Promised Land), though his family didn't really possess it until 400 years later, until after their time in Egypt (a sort of death), and did not receive the city of Jerusalem from God until many years after that. In Hebrews, that story is being used symbolically of course: we can, in a sort of way, arrive at the promise, at what is over the horizon, at what is hoped for; and yet we do not really arrive until we have gone down into Egypt and returned, until we have been destroyed and remade, died and been brought back from the dead. I think that the author of Hebrews is thinking of the fact that in one way we have received the promise, in one way the Kingdom has come. We are no longer simply groping in the dark. In a sort of way, in Jesus Christ the promise is fulfilled, the Kingdom is established – in an odd sort of way, mysteriously, in the way we call 'sacramentally'. Sacramentally, we have arrived at the Kingdom, just as Abraham arrived as a stranger, a foreigner in the Promised Land. But he lived there in a tent – a temporary shack. And he didn't make the mistake of thinking that what he built was the real thing. It was just a structure he threw up while waiting for the gift of the real city, waiting for the terrible giving of the city, a giving that involved letting his people be broken and remade.

In a way the whole thing is a bit like growing up, becoming mature, becoming in fact fully human. I'm not saying that adults are always more human than children, certainly not that they are always better than children. But the thing that education, maturing, growing up is supposed to be for is to develop your humanity. Of course children already possess humanity. But it is also something they are reaching towards, something unknown. They must live in their childhood as in a tent, as in a temporary dwelling. They must not cling to it as a permanent possession. If they do, it becomes a hiding-place, a way of avoiding the call to set out and grow up. But obeying that call means not only venturing into the unknown. It means venturing into the unexpected. It means being prepared to let the tent be blown away by the wind of the Spirit. It means what they call the crisis of adolescence, when you were destroyed and remade (well or badly as the case may be).

Now the Church, and any other structures we use on our way to the Kingdom, or when we first arrive in the Kingdom, are all tents, shacks. But we *can* treat them as permanent. And then they become hiding-places, ways of evading the summons to receive the real city from the terrible hands of God, ways of refusing to be taken down into Egypt and remade, ways of refusing death and, therefore, of refusing resurrection.

For faith is about the way we get to the Promised Land in the most unexpected and least likely way. Not the prudent and reasonable way, but the very opposite. The Promised Land is like the child Isaac, impossibly born of the barren Sarah and the aged Abraham. It is like Jesus born of the Virgin Mary. It is like Isaac given back from the dead. It is like Jesus crucified and raised from the dead. It *is* Jesus crucified and raised from the dead.

Faith is about what is beyond the horizon of the humanly possible. Faith is exploring into what people could never achieve by themselves. Faith is the mysterious *need* in us to get to where we could surely *never* go. Faith, in fact, is about what we call God. Faith is the inkling that we are meant to be divine, that our journey will go beyond any horizon at all into the limitlessness of the Godhead. Faith is not *our* power to set out on this journey into the future. It is our future laying hold on us. It is the crucified and risen Christ gathering us toward himself. Faith is not something we possess. It is something by which we are possessed. It is the Spirit of Christ bringing us to what we are meant for: the eternal love which is the Father.

Chapter 2

Hope

1 PRAYER

Give us this day ...

I am going to begin by talking about prayer, because prayer, asking God to do things for us, is the first way we show that we have hope, trust in God for our future. The season of Advent (the four weeks before Christmas) is all about hope; it is the time for celebrating our confidence that God will come to us to heal us and to help us, our confidence that God is coming to heal the whole world and bring it to the Kingdom of God.

In this first section I don't want to talk about God's plan for the whole of human history, but just about his plan for me and for each of you. And so I am going to talk about personal praying which is, first of all, asking God that his plan should go one way for you and not another. It is asking God that his plan should include you or your friend recovering from sickness or passing an exam or being able to keep up with the mortgage payments. There are some puzzling things about prayer. That is why I want to talk about it.

First of all, surely God knows better than we do what is good for us. He is wise enough and loving enough to take charge of our lives without our offering advice and clamouring for what *we* want. Jesus said, 'Your father knows what you need before you ask him', so what is the point of trying to teach him? Well, your Father does know what you need before you ask him; but

5

do you? Moreover, it is also Jesus who has the nerve to compare his Father answering your prayer to a man who is shouted at and pestered by a neighbour in the middle of the night until he reluctantly gets out of bed and gives him what he wants.

But it does seem odd that God should need to be goaded by our nagging before he is ready to give us his gifts.

Well, try turning that on its head: maybe *we* need to express and recognize our desires, by pleading with God, before we are ready to accept his gift – I mean accept it as his *gift*, as a sign of his love. The prayer is not to make God ready to give, but to make us ready to receive. Have you ever said 'thank you' for a gift by saying, 'It's just what I've always wanted'? Well, God wants his gifts to be, and to be seen to be, what we have *wanted*. After all, every good thing that comes to us is the gift of God; but when it comes to us as an answer to prayer we see it for what it really is, as a gift of God, an expression of his love. Every healing brought about by the skill of doctors and nurses, and every single one of the wonders of medical treatment, is brought about by God who holds all of them in being. He holds in being the skill of the doctors and nurses and the power of the healing drugs. The hand of God is in the hands of the surgeon and the nurse, in everything good and positive that is done. But God is *so* present in everything in our world that we can easily forget him; we can think just of the natural causes of things, forgetting that they are all instruments of God's love, that their acts are all divine acts. In Galilee, in the power of God, Jesus multiplied the loaves, but the power of God was just as much in the growing of the barley and the baking of the bread – only we might not notice it there. It is when good things come to us in an answer to prayer that we take notice of the hand of God and we respond to his love with our love and gratitude – and that is good for us and that is why God wants us to pray.

In prayer, then, we do not want to change God's mind, to bring him round to our way of thinking and wanting. Rather it is God who wants us to change our minds, to attend to what he has given, to recognize him, to believe in him and love him and be grateful to him as our loving Father.

Remember that prayer itself is also one of the good things that God brings into being and holds in being. Our praying itself is as much God's gift as is the answer to it. And prayer is not just God's gift in the way that our power of speech or our health is God's gift; prayer is God's *grace*, and that means it is due to God's own life within us, God's own spirit within us. For God gives us not just our marvellous human powers and skills; he gives us himself, makes us able to live by his own divine life through his Son, Jesus Christ.

When we pray, we display a divine power which is in us because we are in Christ, sharing his life. We speak to the Father with the voice of his Son because we have been taken up to share in their Spirit. The great prayer, the first prayer, was the cross, when Jesus, for the sake of his fellow men and women, accepted total failure, crucifixion and death and left it all to the will of his Father. This was the prayer that was answered in the resurrection of Jesus and the redemption of the world. Whenever we pray it is because in Christ we are linked with that prayer; whenever we pray we share in that prayer, the prayer of the cross. Especially, of course, when we celebrate the sacrament of the cross, the sign of the cross, as we do in the eucharist, but also whenever we pray. *Whenever*. And *whatever* we pray for, we are in Christ.

Now this is an astonishing teaching: every bringing of our desires before our Father in heaven is Christ in us speaking to his Father and ours. There are people, you know, who cannot believe this. They will tell you that the only true prayer is prayer for higher spiritual things, unselfish prayer, prayer for the grace to be forgiving and kind, for a deeper understanding of the scriptures, for the conversion of sinners, prayer for others and not for ourselves. They are very shocked if you say that praying to pass an exam or, worse still, praying that you will be able to afford a new car, is just as much part of the life of the Spirit.

You must indeed pray for the right things; but the right things are not the noble high-minded things that you think you *ought* to want, they are the vulgar and rather infantile things you really *do* want. Genuine prayer means honest prayer, laying before your Father in heaven the actual desires of your heart – never mind how childish they may sound. Your Father knows how to cope with that.

People often complain of 'distractions' during prayer. Their mind goes wandering off on to other things. This is nearly always due to praying for something you do not really much want; you just think it would be proper and respectable and 'religious' to want it. So you pray high-mindedly for big but distant things like peace in Northern Ireland or you pray that your aunt will get better from the flu – when in fact you do not much care about these things; perhaps you ought to, but you don't. And so your prayer is rapidly invaded by distractions arising from what you really do want – promotion at work, let us say. Distractions are nearly always your real wants breaking in on your prayer for edifying but bogus wants. If you are distracted, trace your distraction back to the real desires it comes from and pray about these. When you are praying for what you really want you will not be distracted. People on sinking ships do not complain of distractions during their prayer.

Never mind then if your prayer seems 'selfish' or childish. If you will be honest in prayer, acknowledging that you are not very altruistic, that you *do* worry about your own interests, if you will just try to be, and admit to being, as you *are*, the Holy Spirit, I promise you, will lead you into a deeper under-standing of who you are and what you really want. For prayer is not only a matter of asking, it turns out to be about learning as well, about growing up, about discovering yourself. When you lay your desires, your *true* desires, before God, you begin to see them in better perspective. Quite often you find that they are not, after all, the things you really want most of all. If you bring these desires out into the light, not only the light of day

8

but the divine light, the light of the Lord, you begin to see them as important but not the *most* important thing to you. And so through the *practice* of praying, God will often lead you nearer and nearer to realizing that in the end what you want most of all is God himself. But that is the end, and this is only the road to it. There is no bypass. We all start as children and we all need time to grow up. It is no good pretending that we are already there. If you treat a 5-year-old as an adult she will never be allowed to grow into a real adult. If you treat yourself as a saint you will never become one; you will never even really want to become one.

Growing up is not, of course, easy. We have to go through times of darkness and bafflement and regression. And this happens in praying too. There is no such thing as an unanswered prayer; and God never gives us less than we ask. When he simply gives us what we ask he is treating us as children and we can rejoice in that. But when he does not he is giving us a greater gift, inviting us to grow a little, to realize not just that there are greater and more important things, but that we actually *want* these more important things. The answer he has given us is just a little bigger than what we first asked for, and it can be very disturbing and painful to adjust to a new understanding of ourselves and our desires.

This, then, is how the infinite unconditional love of God takes us through our life-stories; not usually with thunderbolts and dramatic crises, but gently and gradually leading us into the light, sometimes stumbling, sometimes uncomprehending, but all the time growing and finding ourselves, finding what it means to be in Christ, to be filled with the Spirit, to be children of our Father in heaven.

Come, let us go up to the mountain of the Lord to the house of the God of Jacob that he may teach us his ways that we might walk in his paths. Come let us walk in the light of the Lord.

2 ACTION

Thy kingdom come ...

I have been talking about hope in our personal lives, about how our prayer expresses our hope, our trust and confidence in God who has our life-story in his hands. I now want to move on to a wider stage, to ask not only about *my* future but about *our* future and the future of our children. I want to move from biography, the story of individual lives, to history, the story of whole societies. What hope can there be in a world of disease and famine and, above all, in a world of war – a world of nuclear war?

There are, of course, people who say that Christians, as Christians (and especially Christian ministers and priests), should have no concern with these things. There are people who think that clerics who speak out politically should attend to the services in their churches and leave social and political matters to the politicians who understand them. As church people, they say, we should get on with the business of praying and praising God – if we do have views about political or economic matters it is because we claim some sort of secular expertise. It has nothing to do with our Christianity.

The trouble with this line of talk is that the only God that we pray to and worship says he is very much concerned with economic matters; he says he is the God of the poor. He says he is the God of the righteous, and that means taking sides with the helpless and the downtrodden, with the widow and the orphan, against their oppressors. The God who meets us in the Bible, and ultimately meets us in Jesus of Nazareth, tells us that we cannot be with him, we cannot honestly worship him or speak truly of him, unless we are in solidarity with the poor – nor can we solve any of the world's real problems. Without this commitment to the poor, no amount of expertise will be of the slightest use – quite the contrary. It is not as though we were simply faced with a series of natural disasters like earthquakes or drought. Most of our troubles are man-made, and even when they are unavoidable accidents they are made far worse than they need be by human action or inaction. Nuclear war was invented by experts; poverty is ultimately man-made. We all know that the earth can produce enough food, and more than enough food, to feed everyone on earth. We have famine in the midst of plenty because we have devised a way of living that keeps the food supply away from those who need it. Famine is not a shortage of food: it is a shortage of justice. And in the Bible that means a shortage of concern for the poor.

Of course, it is not that there are wicked men who want people to die of starvation. Nobody, or very few people, actually want children to be slowly burned alive with phosphorous jelly clinging to their skin. But chemical companies do make a profit from manufacturing napalm. Not many people want even their worst enemies to die the hideous deaths that come by nuclear fall-out. But all the same, these are not natural disasters. They happen because of what people want. These things do not happen because people are ill-informed or stupid; they happen because we want to grab for ourselves and because we do not even consider the consequences for others until it is too late. There are even those who think that organized greed is and should be the motivating force of society, that unless people are intelligently greedy there will be no 'progress' – and by progress they mean people (some people) getting richer. But this turns out to be accompanied by a vast number of people being hungry and poor; it is accompanied by regimes of oppression and torture; it is accompanied by wars in which 20 million people have died since 1945. When these accompanying horrors are noticed, it is thought that we have on our hands some complex technical problems that experts will solve so as to leave everything else as it is.

If the world invites us to despair, it is not because of a conspiracy of especially evil people (though I think there are especially evil people). It is certainly not because of some incomprehensibly evil men in the Kremlin, or the Pentagon, or even the Vatican. It is mainly because of the accumulation and interdependence of many small failures, failures of generosity and courage. It is a fact that my minor self-indulgences, my unthinking cruelties, my doctoring of the truth do link up with, and reinforce, the injustice of the world. If the world invites us to despair, it is largely because of our ordinary, undramatic selfishness.

But it is also true, that if we are invited to hope, it is because of a human being too: it is because of the human life, death, resurrection and presence of Jesus Christ. It is because of the power of this man Christ in us, because of the power of the Spirit, that we shall overcome the world.

Do not imagine that I am trying to make you feel guilty for the sin of the world. Not at all: we have been rescued from such guilt and slavery to sin; that is the redemption that Christ won for us on the cross by his loving obedience to his Father's will. The trouble for most of us is that having been rescued from the sin of the world, having escaped from guilt and slavery, we now have a task: we have a fight on our hands.

We are no longer hopeless or helpless, slaves of sin, but our old slave-master is now our *enemy*, whom in the power of the Spirit we have to fight. We have to be engaged in a struggle. For most of us it is not that we have gone over to the enemy (though that can happen); it is just that we do not fight hard enough, and that fight is above all the struggle on behalf of Christ's poor, the oppressed, the helpless. They say Christian preachers should not play at politics. I say we do not have to. There are plenty of Christians who have no interest at all in politics; but if their Christianity is real, the politicians are going to have to be interested in *them*. Nobody nowadays thinks that Jesus was a political activist concerned with political power, but the people who did have political power, the temple priesthood and the Roman colonial authorities, were very concerned about him: they knew that he was a threat, they had him crucified because he was a threat.

Do not imagine that when the world sees how these Christians love one another, it will be lost in admiration. When it sees how these Christians love one another, the world usually goes for its gun. As Jesus promised: the world will hate you. I am talking of course, of the real love that expresses itself in action, not in inane cheerfulness, or a feeling of benevolence.

Of course every society is some attempt by human beings to live together in friendship, in cooperation, and to this extent is a good and God-given thing. The trouble is that we build friendship with some at the expense of others. The democracy of Athens floated on a sea of slaves. The wealthy make a society in which there is a kind of friendship and cooperation but a society from which the poor are excluded – that is why they *are* poor. And because they are excluded they have to be kept down, kept in their place, by fear and lies and force. The precarious stability of 'civilization as we know it' would be profoundly threatened by a serious outbreak of love.

This is the threat posed almost unconsciously and sometimes quite reluctantly by the Christian movement. For Christians – whatever peculiar political prejudices they may have – in the end simply cannot swallow the idea that some group of people are less human, less fit for human society, than others. In the end – and it may take them a very long time to get to this end – their deep conviction is that people matter because they are brothers and sisters of Jesus Christ, that they are all without exception called to be children of God in Christ. This means that however we may twist and turn to keep in with the people in power, however hard the churches may even *try* to sell out to the wealthy and their agents, to collude with the oppressors of the poor – it cannot be done for long. In the end the Church lives by the Holy Spirit and the gates of hell cannot indefinitely prevail. For this we have nowadays the testimony of the men of power themselves: throughout the world, whether it be the businessmen and military dictators of Latin America or the bureaucrats of Eastern Europe, they all agree that the major internal threat to their power comes not from terrorists or political subversives but from those churches that have recovered their Christianity, that have returned to the gospel. Those who have remembered that the Church is just humankind being drawn towards the Kingdom, and that the Kingdom belongs to the poor. It is these churches that are especially hated by the powers of this world.

That is why the Christian hope we celebrate is not *optimism*. Of course we do not believe in the superstition of 'inevitable progress' – which just means that some people will get richer while the world becomes a more fearful and more fearsome place. But we also do not optimistically imagine that the way forward could be simple for men of goodwill.

What we have is not optimism, but hope. We believe that humankind can and will by the power of the Spirit become not ever wealthier but more richly human, less frightened, more free, more secure in the peace that comes from justice and friendship; but only through overcoming the world in Christ. We *can* move to a society, a world, which while not itself, of course, the Kingdom of God, would be on the way to it and would be our best available picture of it. We are not optimistic about the prospect for such a world; we do not have the illusion that justice and peace can be established if only we can find the right technique. We know that quite small attempts to bring about justice, quite small movements of opposition to genocide, racism, war and exploitation meet with blank hostility – first with suspicion and then with persecution. There are large parts of the world where really to make the option for the poor is to invite death-squads and the torture chambers of the police – and there are other parts of the world where things have not come to *such* extremes.

We are not optimists; we do not present a lovely vision of the world which everyone is expected to fall in love with. We simply have, wherever we are, some small local task to do, on the side of justice, for the poor. This, in the power of the Spirit, we will try to do, and we know that to do it is to risk hostility and persecution as Jesus risked crucifixion. It is to risk defeat.

And this is what we mean by hope. For our hope is the kind that goes through defeat and crucifixion to resurrection. We know that we shall sometimes *have* to fail rather than betray the very justice that we struggle for; we shall have to fail rather than use the weapons of the oppressor against him, but we can do this because we have hope, because we know that God will bring life out of such defeat and failure as he brought life out of the tomb of Jesus.

3 SIN

Forgive us our trespasses ...

In the first section we thought about prayer: the expression of hope in our personal lives. Then we looked at hope in a wider sense of hope for the whole world and the coming of the Kingdom. Now we are going to look at hope in connection with our twin enemies: sin and death. I want to talk about the forgiveness of sin: contrition as an expression of hope. In the final section we shall discuss grief for the dead: mourning as an expression of hope. To put it another way: this section is about God being angry with us; the next will be about us being angry with God.

Take this scenario: I sin and so I offend God. He is angry with me, and I fear the wrath of God. Then I kneel before him and beg for his forgiveness, saying that I know that I have done wrong and do not deserve his friendship; but will he take me back all the same? Then the wrath of God is appeased; he changes his mind and is no longer angry with me.

Now this is a perfectly good story, or picture, of God and ourselves. If we are going to imagine God at all we should sometimes imagine him as very angry – especially angry about injustice to his special people: the poor and helpless. This is a very important image of God, but it is only one image. We have to set this image alongside the image of the God who endlessly accepts us, the God who endures our sins and forgives us all the same. We need many images, especially conflicting images. We need lots of images lest we suppose that any of these images *is* God, lest we worship any one of them. We probably all know people who worship the idol of the punitive God; and others whose idol is simply sentimental. If we suppose that God is literally first wrathful and then relenting, we just have two idols, one after the other.

The fact is that the God of wrath and the God who relents are both good but inadequate images, merely pictures of the unfathomable, incomprehensible love which is God.

If we are going to understand anything about the forgiveness of sin we cannot just be content with pictures; we have to *think* as clearly as we can. First of all, we need to make the same kind of somersault as we did about prayer. We have to turn the story on its head. The initiative is always literally with God. When God forgives our sin, he is not changing *his* mind about us; he is changing *our* mind about him. He does not change; his mind is never anything but loving; he *is* love. The forgiveness of sin is God's creative and re-creative love making the desert bloom again, bringing us back from dry sterility to the rich luxuriant life bursting out all over the place. When God changes your mind in this way, when he pours out on you his Spirit of new life, it is exhilarating, but it is also fairly painful. There is a trauma of rebirth as perhaps there is of birth. The exhilaration and the pain that belong to being reborn is what we call contrition, and this is the forgiveness of sin. Contrition is not anxious guilt about sin; it is the continual recognition in hope that the Spirit has come to me *as healing my sin*.

So it is not literally true that because we are sorry God decides to forgive us. That is a perfectly good story, but it is only a story. The literal truth is that we are sorry because God forgives us. Our sorrow for sin just *is* the forgiveness of God working within us. Contrition and forgiveness are just two names for the same thing, they are the gift of the Holy Spirit; the re-creative transforming act of God in us. God does not forgive us because of anything he finds in us; he forgives us out of his sheer delight, his exuberant joy in making the desert bloom again.

In the New Testament, the opposite of love is not hate but fear. Let me explain what I mean. You know how it is with a child who has been deprived of love by her parents and others. She has not been told, and shown, that she matters to others, so she finds it difficult to believe that she matters at all. She works hard at seeming to matter, seeming to be important. To prove that she is someone, she avidly accumulates things, possessions that are *hers*; but deep beneath it all is an anxiety, a feeling that at the centre of her being there is really nothing at all. She lives in fear – not a sensible, rational fear of things or people that may be harmful, but an irrational, generalized fear that there is nothing to her. Because she finds nothing to love in herself, she finds it hard to love others. Others are dangerous; she must put up barriers to protect herself. She will not take delight in people or things unless she possesses them. For her, importance is found not in the real world that God has made but in a world of fantasy that she has made. And all the time she is deeply aware of how fragile this fantasy world is, how precarious this fantasy self is. That is why above all she is terrified of admitting that she has been wrong – admitting it to others or to herself.

I hope that it is clear that I am talking about most of us; there is some of this anxiety and this fantasy in nearly everyone.

I say all this not to pose as a psychologist; it seems to me just common sense. I mention it because I think it makes a very good image of what Christians mean by sin. Of course it is not sin, but it is an *image* of sin. The root of all sin is fear: the very deep fear that we are nothing; the compulsion, therefore, to make something of ourselves, to construct a self-flattering image of ourselves we can worship, to believe in ourselves – our fantasy selves. I think that all sins are failures in being realistic; even the simple everyday sins of the flesh, that seem to come from mere childish greed for pleasure, have their deepest origin in anxiety about whether we really matter, the anxiety that makes us desperate for self-reassurance. To sin is always to construct an illusory self that we can admire, instead of the real self that we can only love. It is because we fail in realistic self-love that we fail in love for others. So sin, too, means being terrified of admitting that we have failed. In the New Testament sin is represented, first of all by those who dare not know that they are sinners, the self-righteous, the people we call the 'pharisees' (which is, of course, deeply unfair to the real Pharisees), the people obsessed with proving themselves good or 'the elect'.

The cure for this, of course, is to discover that it is all right; we don't have to worry, because God loves us; we do matter because we matter to God. This is what we mean by faith: to realize that the most important thing about us, the deepest thing in us, is that we are loved, unconditionally, never-failingly loved, by God. The gift of faith in God's love for us, the gift of a share in God's own way of seeing things, liberates us from all that tedious business of putting on a show for ourselves or others. We don't need to keep on justifying ourselves any more; we can admit to being the inadequate and rather unpleasant people, and certainly infantile people, that we really are; because it doesn't matter – God loves us anyway. And once we have seen this, once we have been liberated, once in the Spirit of God we find the courage to face our real selves, then at last we can grow up a bit; the perfect love of God for us has cast out fear, we can grow in the life of the Spirit. One of the first signs of the divine life in us is that we can confess our sins.

In one way to face our sins for what they are is more painful, certainly more embarrassing, than to hide from them – as I said, contrition is painful as well as exhilarating – but we are no longer frightened of them; we can see ourselves as comic figures – everyone who takes himself too solemnly is a bit ridiculous. And this too is to share in God's own way of seeing things. Alongside that image of the God of wrath and the God who relents, we surely also need the God who is amused by his

18

wayward children – especially when they are being very pompous and solemn.

I have hope, then, although I am not a saint, because I believe God loves me and forgives me by the gift of contrition, that he continually brings me back to reality, to the truth of things. Of course I do not imagine that God has waved a magic wand so that sin is no longer a threat to me. My contrition, my joy in being forgiven, goes with a realistic understanding that while, of course, there is no danger that any power could drag me back to the world of shadows, of sin and illusion and self-worship, nothing could drag me back there, I could, if I worked at it, go back there myself. Our hope, as I said in the last section, is very different from optimism. Just as there is no automatic mechanism by which we are bound to progress regardless of how we struggle, so there is no automatic salvation regardless of our growth in the life of the Spirit. The grace of God will never reject us, but we can, if we really want to, reject the grace of God. We can want some possession for ourselves so badly that we will even sacrifice for it the friendship of God. Yet even then perhaps God may bring us his gift of sorrow, of contrition, of real faith in his love, of forgiveness so that we may set forth again and

> The desert shall rejoice and blossom . . .
> And we shall come to Zion with singing;
> everlasting joy shall be upon our heads;
> we shall obtain joy and gladness
> and sorrow and sighing shall flee away.

4 DEATH

Deliver us from evil . . .

Christmas is the season of festivity and joy, the feast of warmth and light and life in the midst of winter; so I want to talk about death.

I am not just being perverse for, as we shall see, the hope that we celebrate in Advent has a great deal to do with death. But, in any case, although the shop windows and the advertisers will not let us think about it much, Christmas is in many ways a season of death. I am told that there are more suicides at Christmas than at other times of the year. I think that the gaiety and glitter that we associate with Christmas can make it a very bitter time for lonely people who have no parties to go to and no relatives to visit and feast with. It is also a time when many old people die from what we call 'natural causes' – which quite often means that we have deprived them of enough money to keep them warm. But besides all this, Christmas is also a time when we remember most poignantly friends who have died, who are not there as they used to be to join in the feast. Two very close friends of mine died earlier this year and I know that I am going to miss them particularly at Christmas. Surprisingly, Christmas can be time of mourning just because it is a time of celebration.

So I want to talk a bit about death and about mourning. I want to talk about why we should be angry about death. I want to suggest that just as at the centre of our sorrow for sin we discover forgiveness, so we can discover at the centre of our grief a hope in resurrection.

Death, human death, is in the first place an outrage. I mean it is outrageous in a way that the death of other animals is not; because in human death nature takes back more that it has lent to us. Every human death is a kind of murder.

Put it this way: as every cat-person knows, each cat is a unique individual, different from every other cat. But it is unique because of what it has received from nature, from its genetic make-up and from what has happened to it during its life. When a cat dies, this unique life is no more; this is of course sad, but nature has simply taken back what it has given. I can grieve for the death of a cat, but with the death of a friend there is something much more, something of a different kind; we have an instinct that finds the death of a friend somehow unfair, outrageous, and I think we are right to trust this instinct. For my friend is a unique irreplaceable person not just because of what she has received from nature but because of what she herself has made of herself by her own free decisions, by the spontaneous love she had, by her failings, by all the things that we could praise or blame her for. Unlike the cat, my friend was in part responsible for herself; in a way she created the kind of person she was; she was not just made, she also made herself. She belonged to herself, she was not just a part of nature. And now, in the natural course of things, the lifetime of a body has come to an end; but nature, in claiming back her own, has also taken away the unique personality of that body – which nature did not give.

There are people who will pretend to see death as quite natural, as natural as birth; but I think they should look again. Human life, unlike other life, is more than a simple cycle of birth, growth, maturity, decline and death; during and within this cycle there is a story, there is the development of a person which is not a cycle but a continuing story that is arbitrarily cut off by death. Most people will agree that there is something shocking in the death of a child, who has not had a chance even to live out her whole human life-cycle; but I think that, in one way, every human death is the death of a child: every death cuts off a story that has infinite possibilities ahead of it.

Human love is about bodies, about being with each other, about bodily, physical presence to each other. Those who love find it hard to be separated from each other, even for a few weeks, even by a few miles. They will try to communicate, which is a way of trying to be bodily present. Death is terrible because it is so absolutely a bodily separation, the final bodily absence. What had been a living body, in which a unique personality was present to you, is not a human body any more; it is lifeless clay.

We are right to be angry about death; and anger is a large part of mourning for the dead. And we are right to be angry with God. It is just as appropriate to be angry with God as it is to beg his forgiveness or to ask him for anything in prayer. Of course God does not literally need to be told what we want and need, but, as we saw earlier, it still makes sense to lay our desires before God. Similarly, of course, God is not literally blameworthy, but it still makes sense for us to lay our anger before him. Remember that in all these cases we are dealing with images of God; and in all these cases the literal truth is that the initiative is always with God. What is happening is not happening to God but to ourselves, by the initiative of God's grace. As we saw in the previous section, we need, besides the image of the God who is relenting, also the image of the God who is angry at injustice; and now I say we also need the image of the God with whom we can be angry. If you think this is shocking and irreligious, go back to the Bible, read the psalms, read Jeremiah, read the angry words of Jesus on the cross: 'My God, my God, why have you forsaken me?'

If we suppress our anger at death, if we do not allow ourselves to mourn (or if society or the Church will not allow us to mourn) we will pretend to ourselves that there is no death – and then we shall not cope with it. To pretend that death is unreal is to be very close to those who pretend they have no sin, the self-righteous. As we have seen, contrition is a kind of mourning for sin; it goes with confession, with being able to admit that we are sinners and that nonetheless God loves us and forgives us. It is one and the same gift of God for us to admit to our sin in sorrow and for it to be forgiven; it is one and the same gift of God to mourn for the reality of death and to have hope in the resurrection.

Those who cannot admit the reality of death sometimes convince themselves that we are not really these bodily material animals. The real me, they think, is not this body but a 'spiritual' soul loosely attached to the body. This true 'spiritual' me does not die; it just carries on when the body disintegrates. This disowning of our bodies leads to philosophical muddles, psychological troubles and very bad theology. I am this material animal that God has made. True, I am this special kind of animal that God has created able to make itself, to be creative and free, but I am not some idealized spirit 'harnessed to a dying animal'; I am this dying animal.

I have hope beyond death, not because I think I am a phantom constitutionally incapable of death, but because the bodily animal Jesus Christ has conquered death.

Philosophers have sometimes argued that there is an immortal element in me, a part of my life that does not die; and they may well be right (in fact, I usually think they are right). Of course this soul would not be me; what I am is this whole, living, breathing, thinking animal; but perhaps some of what it is for me to live humanly and creatively is not subject to decay. But, anyway, I do not hope because of what philosophers argue, any more than I have faith because of what philosophers argue.

I have hope because God raised Jesus from the dead and I am promised resurrection and eternal life in him. Jesus was not immortal; he was a mortal man and died; but God conquered death in him and now he has a new immortal bodily life. And because he is not dead, because he is bodily, he can be with us truly and humanly in the body.

To try to understand the resurrection, or rather to try to cope with the fact that we cannot understand it, we need to go back to what we saw about so-called unanswered prayer.

You may remember that I said that all our prayer is a kind of sharing in the great prayer which is the cross, when Jesus in loving obedience accepted failure and handed his whole work over to his Father. This was the prayer that was answered by his resurrection and the redemption of the world.

Now when we die in faith we share in the death of Jesus, we share in the prayer which is the cross, and we share in the answer to that prayer.

You may remember that I said there is no such thing as unanswered prayer; God never gives us less than we ask. But sometimes he gives us so much more than we ask that we do not yet recognize it as an answer at all. Sometimes, it is true, he treats us as children and gives us simply what we ask, and that is easy and delightful; but sometimes he gives us a greater gift and begins to show us that we want something greater. He helps us to grow up. At times the divine power does answer the prayer for life by giving us just exactly what we ask, as when the dead are brought back to life, like Lazarus; but usually he gives us far more; he gives us resurrection which is more than we can yet understand; more than we know enough to ask for.

Like so-called unanswered prayer, death is also a process by which we learn or grow up. The gift of resurrection looks to us now like a prayer that has been ignored, because we are not yet grown up enough to recognize it as what we really want. But if through our lives we have prayed we know how often we have seen by hindsight how what looked like a prayer unheard was a prayer answered in ways that we could not at the time understand. It will be so with our resurrection: we shall look back and see that our new transfigured human life is really what the prayer of our death was all for; just as the resurrection of Jesus was what the prayer of Gethsemane and the cross was all for.

But meantime let us not pretend that for most of us death seems little more than darkness and loss. Yet it is a darkness in which we have hope. Christians have no theory about life after death; we do not think we are old enough to understand such eternal life; we have instead our faith in the love of the Father, our faith in Jesus Christ, that the Spirit of love in us will conquer death and our future is the substance of things hoped for.

Chapter 3

Motorways and God

When the M40 motorway comes to the Chiltern Hills, it doesn't really climb them. It slices straight through. And when it comes to the valley of High Wycombe, it doesn't go down to it. It strides across on stilts. It never turns any sharp corners. It goes on in a more or less straight line. And its surface is kept smooth, with no bumps on it to speak of. When they built it they must (cf. Isaiah 40:4) have said to themselves:

> Every valley shall be lifted up,
>   and every mountain and hill shall be made low;
> the uneven ground shall become level,
>   and the rough places a plain.

Think how very different all this is from the old-fashioned kind of road, the winding lane, Chesterton's rolling English road that the English drunkards made. The old road climbs cautiously up the hills with many loops and bends. Then it swoops down into the valley. Often, when it comes to some great property, some important landed estate, it turns and creeps apologetically right round it. It tries to find the most convenient way through the countryside that it encounters. It follows the contours. It responds to the terrain that it has to go through.

Now this old-fashioned sort of road is an image of the way *we* deal with each other, how we *have* to deal with people. With

25

people we don't like much, it is often an uphill struggle. It is difficult to get to know them, and we approach them as we climb a hill – with bends and loops and changes of tactics as we try to respond to them. With our *friends* it is all so much easier: a downhill run that carries us along. With *powerful* people that we are afraid of, we avoid them if we can; we creep right round them and hope we won't be seen. We often have to make sudden twists and turns, and sometimes we double back. The going is rough quite a lot of the time. We have to assess people all the time. We have to judge them to see whether they are friendly, hostile, or uncaring, so that we can measure our best response to them, or perhaps decide not to respond at all. Are they going to be helpful? Or will they just make things worse? All this is a bit like the old kind of road, cautiously picking its way through the terrain, careful to make the appropriate decision.

'My thoughts are not your thoughts, nor are your ways my ways, says the Lord' (Isaiah 55:8). God's way is very much simpler than our ways. He doesn't have our complications. He is just simply in love with us. Not just with some of us, not just with saints or people who try to be good, but with absolutely everybody: with liars and murderers, with traitors and rapists, with the greedy, the arrogant, the inconsiderate, with prime ministers and priests and policemen. He loves us all. And not in some general way. It is not a question of some vague warm feeling for humanity, for the human race. You must not think that because God knows us all, he views us as some lofty bureaucrat might do, for whom we are each statistics in some great overall pattern. He loves each of us intimately and personally – more intimately and personally than we can love ourselves. He is more personally concerned for our good and happiness than we can be ourselves.

The way of God's love is more like the motorway. It doesn't care whether it meets easy or difficult, uphill or downhill, good or bad. It doesn't care how important or unimportant we are. All those careful judgements *we* have to make, distinguishing

26

friends from foes, working out just the degree of intimacy that
is desirable in particular cases; all that deciding who is good-
hearted and kindly and candid, and who is mean and self-
seeking, who is virtuous and who vicious, who is a sinner and
who is righteous – none of this counts with God's love. He cuts
straight through all the mountains and the valleys, the heights
of sanctity and the depths of depravity. He does not turn aside
from anyone. His way is smooth and easy and swift. And it
reaches to sinners as well as to saints.

God does not *respond* to his world. He does not adjust his
reaction to suit good people or bad. You do not have to be
good *before* God will love you; you do not have to try to be
good *before* God will forgive you; you do not have to repent
before you will be absolved by God. It is all the other way
round. If you *are* good, it is because God's love has already
made you so; if you *want to try* to be good, that is because God is
loving you; if you *want* to be forgiven, that is because God is
forgiving you. You do not have to do anything, or pay
anything, in exchange for God's love. God does not demand
anything of you. Nothing whatever.

There is just one thing you need: you have to be ready to
take a risk. You have to be ready to be destroyed, for all your
security to crumble. You have to be prepared to let go of that
faith in yourself that you have so lovingly built up, your faith
in what *belongs* to you, your possessions of every kind. You have
to be ready to be taken into the dark abyss of God's love. You
have to have faith in his love; for you face the dreadful danger
of becoming good, of becoming yourself as loving as God is
loving. And this is a frightening prospect. The motorway can
do terrible things to the countryside as it spears through it.
And God's love can do terrible things to you. It may make you
kind and considerate and loving.

Do you remember how Paul describes the catastrophic
effects of love? God's love and forgiveness may make you
patient and kind, not jealous or boastful; it may prevent you
from being arrogant, or rude, or insisting on your own way, or

being irritable or resentful, so that you do not rejoice in wrongs but only in what is right. It may make you bear all things, believe all things, hope all things (cf. 1 Corinthians 13:4–7). Well, you know what happens to people like that: they are patronized, taken advantage of, used and despised. If you want an extreme reminder of the risks you take in being forgiven, in being liberated from sin, in becoming loving, just look at a crucifix.

The crucifix shows us that God does not only love us blindly and unconditionally. It also shows us that he was ready himself to take the risks that we take in being loved by God. The Word of God was made flesh so that he could suffer, suffer at our hands because he was a servant of love. God's love does not come from responding to the world. It is his free and gracious gift. But because God became flesh so that *we* could respond to his love, we could take it out on *him* for daring to love us, daring to threaten us with his love, daring to risk transforming us by his love. This is part of the meaning of the season of Advent culminating in Christmas: that God became flesh so that he could suffer. The mystery of Bethlehem is that God began to feel the cold as he was later to feel the torture instruments and the cross. With the insane unthinking directness of love, he blundered into our lives, crashing through like the motorway, so that he could share the price of being loved that this world exacts. He came to *share* our lives and sufferings in time so that we could share his life of love and joy in eternity.

Chapter 4

Felix Culpa

I have come not to call the righteous, but sinners.
(Matthew 9:13; cf. Mark 2:17 and Luke 5:32)

This, and several other passages in the New Testament, teach a scandalous doctrine: that God cares more about selfish, dishonest, mean, cruel, depraved, criminal people than he does about people who try to lead a decent human life, who are compassionate to those in need, faithful to their vows of marriage, just in their dealings, and so on. The idea seems to be that God cares more about criminals. This teaching is all over the New Testament. Think of the parable of the shepherd who neglects all those docile sheep alone and at risk in the desert and goes after the one gormless brute that has got itself lost (Luke 15:1–6). Think of those in heaven rejoicing more over one sinner that has been brought to repentance than over 99 righteous that do not need repentance (Luke 15:7). And so on.

So far as I know, this scandalous teaching is unique to the Christian gospel. Whatever this may be, it is certainly not just moral advice, though it does make some tough moral demands – such as the one that, like God, we too should love sinners.

The gospel is not about being good; it is about being rescued. It is not about being safe; it is about being saved.

I think we have to recognize that the Christian teaching about sinners is just as much a mystery as the Incarnation or the Trinity or the eucharistic presence of the body and blood of Christ. We can never comprehend or give an explanation of such a mystery. But what, at least, we can do is try to see why Christian doctrines are not necessarily nonsense.

OK then. Our God is the God of righteousness who detests sin. So what is so marvellous about the sinner? And what is so unmarvellous about the righteous person?

Let us clear the ground a bit by thinking about sin. The sinner is the last person to understand that he is a sinner. Sin is invisible to the sinner because all sin begins in self-deception. Sinners may know in an abstract sort of way that what they are doing or failing to do is incompatible with friendship, with that life with each other that is necessary for satisfactory human living. They may worry occasionally that they have in some way cut themselves off from honest relations with others. But what they *say* to themselves is that the money or the power or the pleasure makes it worth it.

I am talking about real sin in the proper sense, which is to choose some perfectly genuine but minor good of this life, like wealth, at the expense of really important goods, like being just or faithful or compassionate. Sin lies in desiring the minor good and failing to desire the great good. When we sin we are not necessarily lusting after evil. But we are always failing to be passionate enough about the things that really matter to us. Real sin is to act in ways that amount to rejecting the whole idea that what matters above all in human life is charity. It is to seek what we want by opting out of the Kingdom of God (the kingdom of charity), for the sake of a trivial good.

This is something different from what is sometimes called 'venial' sin, which is a matter of not being very good at living *in* the kingdom of charity. Venial sins do not diminish our charity or make it grow cooler. Our charity is the life in us of the Spirit of God. And nothing *we* could do could make it grow less. But in real sin (sometimes called 'mortal' sin) we take ourselves out of the kingdom of charity altogether. And then, since we have rejected life in the Spirit of God, there is no way back for us. We can't create the Spirit of God in ourselves. It is as though we had committed suicide. We cannot bring ourselves back to life. Change can only happen by the Spirit coming to us unpredictably and gratuitously to bring us back to life by giving us the beginnings of a desire for life. (In mortal sin we can no more even *desire* to return to life: like a corpse, we do not know that we are dead.) We can only be rescued by the miraculous divine intervention that we call repentance or contrition or forgiveness. These are all names for the same thing. And that thing is the coming of God to save us. And God does not go in for that because he has to, because he is obliged to. If and when God comes to save us, it is because he loves us and for no other reason. Unless and until God acts in this way, sinners are quite oblivious of their condition. They will quite often think of themselves as fairly decent persons (cf. Luke 18:9–14). But they are living on a fundamental self-deception which nothing could cure except the extraordinary advent of God's love and forgiveness. That this should happen is something that is neither probable nor improbable: it is not that kind of event. How probable something is depends on an assessment of the circumstances. And God has no circumstances. The creation of the entire universe could not have been either probable or improbable. Like the forgiveness of sin it is a sheer gratuitous expression of God's love.

The Empress Catherine the Great famously said, 'I shall be an autocrat: that's my *métier*, my trade. And the good Lord will forgive me: that is his trade.' She could hardly have been more wrong; and, of course, she knew it quite well. She was just trying to be shocking. Now Jesus, in his talk about the righteous and sinners, is saying, in effect: it is a *great* thing for the creator's love to bring the whole universe and all that happens in it into existence when there might have been nothing at all; but an even *greater* thing for this gratuitous creative love to convert a creature who actually *rejects* his creator's love into one who shares his creator's own existence. And this is what the forgiveness of sin is.

There is a famous phrase from the traditional hymn of praise that the deacon sings at the Easter Vigil next to the paschal candle. He speaks of the *'felix culpa'*, the happy or fortunate sin of Adam which was the occasion for the forgiveness and salvation of the world in Christ by his cross and resurrection. You might say that God can permit sin, in his mysterious plan sometimes, in order to do the greater thing of forgiving it. *God* may ordain that in this or that case it is in his plan better to have sinned and be forgiven than not to have sinned.

I speak, please notice, of *God's* plan, not of *our* plan. It may be a greater thing to be a forgiven sinner than not to have sinned. But it would make no sense to sin in order to be forgiven into greater sanctity. That would be like Lazarus committing suicide in order to be raised from the dead. Only God, in his gratuitous love, might raise up Lazarus. And only God in his gratuitous, quite unpredictable, love could forgive our sin. This is something *God* might intend. But for us to intend it would be (as with the Empress, if she had not been joking) what we call the sin of presumption.

But sin remains, as I have said, a mystery. And, like all mysteries it is really about the mystery which is God. God evidently could have created a world in which there was no sin at all. I do not think he could have created a material world in which there was no destruction and suffering. Being killed and suffering are necessary features of a natural material world developing in accordance with its own natural laws. In such a world, when the living thing that is prey is diminished or destroyed, the predator is enhanced and survives in that same action. You can see the point of all that. But sin, on the other hand, is completely puzzling. Sin has no point at all in the natural created world; for here it is as though the predator simply ate *itself*. You may sin by damaging others. But what makes it sin is that you are damaging yourself. There is no use for sin. After the resurrection we shall all live, and live more abundantly, without any sin at all. Of course, there are those who think that God had to allow for sin in order that we could exercise our freedom; but this view is preposterous. The assumption behind it is that our freedom somehow lets us *escape* from God – as though we were free *in spite of* God. But, of course, our freedom is the greatest manifestation in us of God's creative love. Our free spontaneous acts really do exist. So they are created and sustained in us by God. God is not a coercive force outside us. He makes us ourselves, and especially ourselves in our freedom. We are not free *in spite of* God but *because of* God. Any other view of God is idolatrous, making God a being within creation, a rival to his free creatures.

There is, it seems to me, no way that God could have needed sin in his world. But in fact there is sin (not, of course, created by God, for sin is not an existing thing but the absence in us of the fullness of humanity), and we can only marvel that in God's plan this sin turns out to have been a *felix culpa*: the happy occasion for the Son of God to be one of us sharing our suffering human nature so that we could be brought out of our sin to share in his divine nature, so that through Christ's human life and death and resurrection we could share in the Spirit, which is the joyful life of the Father, for eternity.

Chapter 5

Abraham and Isaac

There are a lot of things to be said, of one kind and another, about the story of Abraham and Isaac as found in Genesis 22. There are hints in it of a tradition of human sacrifice against which the Hebrews were reacting. It is a story told as a basis for the prescription that the first-born belongs to God and has to be bought back, redeemed, paid for by a ritual gift, and so on. But these are scholarly matters which I want to leave aside for the moment. For now, let's just look briefly at the position of Abraham himself.

God tells him to 'Take your son, your only son Isaac, whom you love ... and offer him ... as a burnt offering on one of the mountains that I shall show you.' Now I think that if we pay too much attention to the remark that Abraham loved Isaac we are in danger of sentimentalizing the story a little. Of course it would be an appalling wrench for Abraham to kill his own son. But there is more to it than that. The central point is that Isaac is his *only* son, and, as is made clear earlier in Genesis, *the only son he is likely to have*. For Abraham to kill Isaac is to cut off any chance of posterity. And in the Hebrew tradition, as in so many others, this would, in some ways, be to reduce his life to unmeaning. A man felt that his significance, the sense of his life, was tied up in being the father of a line. You get the same kind of passionate concern in Shakespeare's *Macbeth*, where the important thing to people seems to be not their own happiness, still less their own comfort, but that they should found a line of kings. I don't think we find this all that easy to understand (I don't anyway), but it is evidently there.

But this isn't the whole of it, not by any means. Isaac is not only Abraham's *son* whom he loves. And he is not only his *only* son, the one chance he has of carrying on his line. He is also the one through whom God *has promised* to carry on his line. In Genesis 21 there is a story in which God says: 'It is through Isaac that offspring shall be named for you.' Here we have a complete contradiction: God promises that through Isaac Abraham will have a long line of descendants, and then God demands that Isaac himself should be killed. This is the baffling position in which Abraham is placed.

Now, of course, the story in Genesis 21 is a separate one from the story of the sacrifice in Genesis 22. And it possibly comes from a different tradition, was told in a different part of the land and was written a good deal later than the sacrifice story. But none of that need concern us at present. The point is that the final editor of Genesis has put these stories together. He presents Abraham as faced with a stark contradiction. The God of Abraham faces him with a complete absurdity. He doesn't just ask him to do something *difficult*, to kill one of his children. He doesn't just ask him to take the meaning out of his life by destroying his last chance of posterity. God asks Abraham to make nonsense of his *own promise*. 'It is through Isaac that offspring shall be named for you ... Take your son, your only son Isaac, whom you love ... and offer him ... as a burnt offering.' And the central point of the story, at least as for example St Paul sees it, looking back from the New Testament, is that Abraham believed God: that in spite of this absurdity he was prepared to follow the word of God.

We ought not, by the way, to be confused by moral considerations at this point. The Hebrews did, of course, protest against child-sacrifice because they believed that it was *forbidden* by God. But they would have had no serious qualms about the morality of a father taking the life of his child if it were *commanded* by God. We should not look at the Old

Testament through our own moral spectacles. Our own protest against child-sacrifice, so widespread a custom in our culture (whether by abortion or acts of war), is of a rather different kind. I mean that most of us would, I suppose, base our protest on universal moral principles: it is undesirable that people should do certain kinds of things to other people. For the Old Testament, however, it is much more directly a matter of the command of God. But that is by the way. Let us return to Abraham and his faith.

God has said clearly that it is by Isaac growing up and having children that Abraham will have his descendants. And now he says: 'Kill Isaac, don't let him grow up.' How could Isaac, having been killed, produce descendants for Abraham? Can a man after his death, rise up and carry on the family line? Abraham didn't know. He couldn't understand it. But he just left the matter to God, trusting, believing in his promise.

Now we are a bit let down at the end of this story. At least I've always felt the ending is a bit banal. God just relents, or he says 'It's all right, I was only testing you. I didn't really mean it.' So Abraham sacrifices the ram instead. (There's a much more interesting ending to Wilfred Owen's poem about the 1914–18 war, in which Abraham has got so fascinated with the ritual sacrifice of war in the name of God that he won't listen to God's word: 'But Abraham would not, and slew his son / And half the seed of Europe one by one.') But, as I say, the story in Genesis seems to end rather lamely with God saying it was all a con. Abraham had passed the test. But the happy ending takes away the mystery, the glimpse into the darkness of God that we begin with.

But, of course, the story is only a rehearsal. At least, we, as Christians, can see it now as only a rehearsal. When Jesus is faced with the same problem, the same contradiction as Abraham, there is no happy ending, or, if there is, both happiness and ending take on a new and mysterious meaning.

Note that Jesus too is faced with a kind of contradiction. In obedience to God's command he is fully and completely human, human in a way that we never achieve, human in a way that it is promised we will be in the Kingdom of God. Because he has this profound humanity in a world that is a good deal less than human, because he has (to put it plainly) this capacity for love in a society that is unloving, ridden by fears and anxieties, two things follow: that he has a mission to transform the world and that he will be prevented from carrying it out. The mission of Jesus is as contradictory as God's two announcements to Abraham. God says: 'Do this', and then takes away the only means of doing it. Jesus was to transform the world by love, and it was this very love that made him completely vulnerable, completely at the mercy of the world. The very centre and meaning and essence of his mission guaranteed that it could not be carried out. The life he had come to bring made it certain that he would die.

How could Isaac, being sacrificed and killed, bring forth Abraham's descendants? How could Jesus, murdered on the cross, bring us his love, his personal presence?

In between Abraham and Jesus we have a poem in the book of Isaiah (Chapter 53) which states the same problem. It is promised that the servant of God will be defeated, despised and rejected by men. In a splendid phrase the poet says:

> By a perversion of justice he was taken away.
> Who could have imagined his future?
> For he was cut off from the land of the living,
> stricken for the transgression of my people.
> They made his grave with the wicked
> and his tomb with the rich,
> although he had done no violence,
> and there was no deceit in his mouth.
> Yet it was the will of the Lord to crush
> him with pain.
> When you make his life an offering for sin
> he shall see his offspring, and shall
> prolong his days.

The poet does not explain how the servant can first of all be killed 'by a perversion of justice' and then 'see his offspring' and 'prolong his days'. He just states it as part of the paradox of being the servant of God, part of the mystery of God. There is, for him, no last-minute substitution of another victim (as in the Genesis story). There is just the mystery that if you are the servant of God you can be destroyed and yet carry on your mission: that you *will* be destroyed *in order to* carry on your mission.

That is the kind of thing that it is to be the servant of God. That is the kind of thing we are talking about when we talk about God.

The New Testament puts the point by saying that Jesus was killed and rose from the dead. We ought to try not to see this as an *explanation* – as though we should say: 'Oh, I see, that's how it was done. Jesus died on the cross, his heart stopped beating; but then he came back to life again.' In a way, that would take us back to the Abraham story. Instead of a substitute victim, there is a substitute death. Evidently it isn't really a death if you are going to come back to life a bit later. I remember a friend of mine saying to me, 'I was in hospital and died last month.' He meant that his heart had stopped and that he had to be revived. But, of course, he did not really die. Part of what we mean by real death is its permanence. If Jesus came back to life in a couple of days, then he was never really dead. The gospels warn us against seeing the resurrection of Jesus as simply a resuscitation that would take the mystery and meaning out of the whole thing. To come back to life might be remarkable, it might be a technically difficult thing to do, but we know just what it would mean. But what might rising from the dead mean?

To say that Jesus rose from the dead is, among other things, to say that in spite of the fact that his love for us in obedience to his mission led to his death – or in fact because his love led to his death – he is still present to us, really present to us, present to us and loving us in his full bodily reality. It is not just that

we remember him or imitate him, or that he lives on in a
religious tradition. The good news is that he rose from the
dead, that he went through real death to a new kind of bodily
life, to a new kind of life *with* us. So that when we encounter
someone who needs us, when we find the hungry and the
imprisoned and the homeless, we can really say that here we
encounter Christ, not in some metaphorical way, but literally.
He personally is with us. The difference between having faith
in the literal bodily resurrection of Jesus and not having such
faith is, at one level, the difference between really discovering
Jesus in the needy and oppressed, and simply thinking that it is
a rather beautiful idea. It is the difference between really
believing, like Abraham, that God asks the impossible of us, to
find life through death, creation through destruction, that God
makes the impossible possible for us, and not believing in God
– thereby making him just some part of the machinery of our
world.

To believe in the resurrection is not to hold the view that
God is so clever that he can even bring a dead man back to life.
It is to believe that, whatever we mean by God, his ways are
dark and mysterious, that he leads us, sends us to life and
meaning, through death and absurdity. To recognize this truth
about the human condition, to see it and be obedient to it, as
were Abraham, the servant in Isaiah, and Jesus, is to begin to
understand what God is about.

Chapter 6

Jesus and the Sons of Zebedee

James and John, the sons of Zebedee, came forward to him and said to him, 'Teacher, we want you to do for us whatever we ask of you.' And he said to them, 'What is it you want me to do for you?' And they said to him, 'Grant us to sit, one at your right hand and one at your left, in your glory.' But Jesus said to them, 'You do not know what you are asking. Are you able to drink the cup that I drink, or be baptized with the baptism that I am baptized with? ... The cup that I drink, you will drink; and with the baptism with which I am baptized, you will be baptized; but to sit at my right hand or at my left is not mine to grant.'

(Mark 10:35–38)

In this story of the encounter of Jesus with James and John, the sons of Zebedee, it is hard not to feel that Jesus is either joking or cheating, or both. They ask him for the top jobs in the new administration. He says, 'But can you go through the kind of suffering that I'm going to endure?' They say, 'Yes we can.' And he says, 'Well, so you shall then; but it won't get you any jobs.' This passage, and the ones surrounding it, are all exploring the curious paradoxes in the Christian idea of victory and triumph and success: notions such as that we gain our life by losing it, that we gain victory by accepting failure, that we come to life through death. So let's have a look at these paradoxes.

When we meet them, our trouble, of course, is that we don't take the losing and failure and death seriously enough. We

41

have a tendency to feel that if there is triumph and victory and resurrection on the other side, if the good news is so good, the bad news can't be so bad. And it is as thinking along these lines that Mark presents the sons of Zebedee.

According to Mark (cf. Chapter 9), these two, James and John, together with Peter, had been witnesses to the Transfiguration of Jesus. They had gone up the mountain and seen Jesus in glory with Moses and Elijah, one on his right and one on his left. On the mountain it was Peter who made an ass of himself by looking to build dwellings to house Moses, Elijah and Jesus (Mark 9:5). It was Peter who wanted to fix the moment of triumph, to keep things like that and to avoid the living-out of the history of suffering and death. Now, in Mark's subsequent story, it is the turn of James and John.

After the Transfiguration they had been for a while in 'the region of Judea and beyond the Jordan' (Mark 10:1). Mark gives us fairly precise geography because he wants us to picture Jesus, after a relatively pleasant and peaceful time, turning to go to Jerusalem, the place where he will be betrayed and tortured and killed. As he sets out to cross the Jordan on the road to Jerusalem, Jesus makes his most explicit prophecy of his suffering and death, just before James and John put their request to him. 'We are going up to Jerusalem, and the Son of Man will be handed over to the chief priests and the scribes, and they will condemn him to death; then they will hand him over to the Gentiles; they will mock him, and spit upon him, and flog him, and kill him; and after three days he will rise' (Mark 10:33–4).

Here at the crossing of the Jordan, maybe as they are standing at the ford where, for Mark, the story of Jesus begins with his baptism by John the Baptist (Mark 1), as they are at the river, the two sons of Zebedee, James and John (the 'Sons of Thunder' as Jesus names them in Mark 3:17) come and make their request.

A fair number of scholars think that James and John, like Simon, and perhaps Peter and Judas, were political activists

42

connected with the militant underground Jewish liberation movement: the Zealots. They are certainly presented as activists with clear and definite ideas about what they wanted to achieve. And they expected to achieve this with Jesus. Jesus has just predicted his death but the bit they really pay attention to is the last phrase: 'after three days he will rise'. Yes, of course the struggle is going to be a painful and terrible one. It will be an agony that will go through death itself. But it will be crowned by victory. Jesus will come into his glory. A new era will dawn. And, this being so, James and John, like all good political activists, are already engaged in the necessary and virtuous human activity of the power struggle. We can only guess at the power struggles in the Early Church that lie behind this bit of Mark's gospel. But the gospel in its finished form isn't propaganda for one side or the other. It isn't (anyway overtly) taking sides in the struggle. It is critically reinterpreting the struggle itself.

So, anyway, they come to Jesus. (Matthew, rather endearingly, has their mother coming and asking for them [Matthew 20:20]; but Mrs Zebedee does not feature in Mark.) They ask that when Jesus comes into his glory they may be the new Moses and Elijah on the right and left hand of Jesus – the places of honour and highest authority.

As so often in Mark, Jesus has to tell his followers that they do not understand what it is all about. Can you, he says, drink the chalice of suffering that I am drinking? Can you go through the terrible baptism that John the Baptist prefigured, without knowing what he was doing, when he baptized me here in the Jordan? Can you go through with the doom that I was marked out for that day? Well of course by the time Mark was written, James at least had already been martyred in Jerusalem, and there is no hesitation in their reply: 'We are able' (Mark 10:39). 'We are ready for the struggle; we can take the necessary suffering. But what we are talking about are the fruits of victory.'

'What I have to give you', says Jesus, 'is the real gift, the gift

43

of sharing in my suffering and death. I just don't have, in the same sense, a victory to give. I am not going to inaugurate the messianic kingdom. I am going to die. And, indeed, you can come with me. We cannot see beyond this death. We know that it will *not* be the final absurdity. We know that the Father will make sense of it all. We know that the Son of Man will rise after three days. But the Father will not make sense of his death in our terms, in terms of this world and its calculations. We can't, so to speak, have a diary or an engagement book with: Friday, on cross; Saturday in tomb; Sunday in heaven. The victory beyond death doesn't belong to the same sequence as the events before death and the death itself. We can't be making plans now for the glory that will happen later.'

But this is exactly what the sons of Zebedee are doing. The trouble is not, as some rather priggish commentators have said, that their plans are 'selfish'. There is nothing necessarily selfish about a power struggle. The trouble is that they are planning at all. It is not that Jesus says to them, 'Oh well, I don't know about that; we'll have to decide these things later.' He says: 'These things don't concern me, and so, still less, should they concern you.' He says: 'Our job is to suffer and die. Our job is to make of our suffering and our death an act of sacrificial love.' It is not that it is selfish to think of the reward to come, to plan for the victory. It is just irrelevant and misleading. The whole point of sacrificial love is that you cast yourself simply and totally on the love of God, leaving things to him. The whole point of the good news of grace is that we don't have to plan or achieve anything: that is God's business.

Of course, Jesus is not just saying that the Father's love will make everything all right in the end (though the Father's love *will* make everything all right in the end). Jesus is saying that it is in *him* and through *him* that the Father's love operates. The Son of Man came to be the ultimate servant, the servant of the whole human race. He came to give his life as a redemption for all of us. It is through and because of his dying and his rising again on the third day that our suffering and our death and our sacrificial love can make sense. It is because of his dying and rising that we too are brought out of death to life.

It is not just that a defeat which is an act of love is a victory. It is a defeat *in Christ* that is a victory. For Jesus Christ, this historical individual, is not only the supreme example of love but the source of all genuine love, of all love that conquers death. We must not just die to ourselves but die *in his death*, be baptized into his death, if we are to rise again, if our sacrifice is to make sense. And this also is how we are to be servants. 'Whoever wishes to become great among you must be your servant', says Jesus (Mark 10:43). And 'servant' here means not just any kind of servant but a servant in Christ's servitude. Jesus is not saying that any servitude is good and any power is bad. He is not even saying that any power struggle is bad. He is asking of us the servitude of love such as he had. He is asking of us the love that he had, the spirit of love that he sends into the world. If we seriously try to give each other this service of love then indeed we will drink the cup that he drinks and be baptized with the baptism with which he is baptized. We will be betrayed and we will suffer. But out of this the spirit which raised up Jesus Christ will raise up our mortal bodies also, not to rule, not to sit on the right hand or the left, but to live in Christ's self-abandoning love for eternity.

Chapter 7

Jesus and Sanctity

In one way (at one level), you could say that as knives are for cutting and pens are for writing, people are for living with each other. Someone might be good at singing, or football, or physiotherapy. But what would make her quite simply good, what would make her a good person, would be a matter of how she lives with others. So the Greek philosophers said that man is the political animal, one who lives in a *polis*, in community with others, in the special kind of community that we call friendship, the special sharing of life with each other, loving each other, that belongs to the animals that talk and think and make decisions freely.

In another way we can say that the aim and purpose of human life is to come to God, who made us for himself, so that our hearts do not rest until they rest in him. All other goods are satisfying, but never completely satisfying. The only complete human satisfaction is to be with God.

What makes the Christian gospel unique is that it proclaims that these two apparently quite different ways of talking are, in the end, saying the same thing. For, as the author of 1 John puts it bluntly: 'Whoever does not love does not know God, for God is love' (1 John 4:8). Or, as we sing in Holy Week, '*Ubi caritas et amor, ibi Deus*' ('Where there is charity and love, *there* is God').

This is not to reduce the gospel to friendliness – going around smiling at everybody. It is to say that (while friendship and love can mean a thousand things) what we are seeking in our community with each other is, at its greatest depth, community with God. In any case, friendship is more than kindness and wishing well to another. It is a way of being with another, of sharing life with another. Friends do not want to be separated. If they have to be apart, they will invent ways of being together. Friendship is a quest for unity.

Jesus tells us that his Father, the one who sent him into the world, the one who laid commands upon him, gave him a mission to fulfil (cf. John 8:18). This Father is doing all this in order that there shall be friendship between Jesus and his disciples, just as there is friendship between the Father and Jesus. The aim is that, just as there is one life shared by the Father and Jesus, so there shall be one life shared by Jesus and his followers. Then there will be one life, the same life, shared between the disciples themselves. The Father's command to Jesus is: 'Be in the world and love your fellow men and women.' In his turn Jesus's command to us is that we in the same way love each other (cf. John 13:34).

So what we hear of Jesus is first of all that he is loved by the Father. And that means that Jesus is a saint. For this is what a saint is: a human being with whom God is in love, with whom God shares his own divine life. What we call grace, or holiness, or godliness is just what it is like to be loved by God, to share in divinity. And Jesus is the *first* saint – not the first saint in history, of course, but the first in the sense that all other saints have their godliness from him. As John says at the very beginning of his gospel: 'the Word became flesh and lived among us ... From his fullness we have all received, grace upon grace' (John 1:14–16). Our grace comes from Christ's grace. We are loved by God because Christ is loved by God.

So sanctity is a matter of being loved. And what we are commanded to do, as Jesus is commanded to do, is to abide in this friendship.

What is it to *abide* in friendship? It is to treat friendship as more important than anything else. We are not abiding in friendship if we prefer something else, if we opt for anything else, even life itself, at the expense of unity with our friend. That is why Jesus goes on to say: 'No one has greater love than this, to lay down one's life for one's friends' (John 15:13). Friendship is finding the *sharing* of life more important than carrying on the individual life. This is what Jesus is saying on the cross: 'It is better to die, sharing the last of my life with the Father, than to make my life a little longer in separation from his life.' This is his obedience to the demands of friendship, friendship with the Father.

Friendship is always *with*. It is always reciprocal. When Jesus consummates his friendship with the Father in his death on the cross, the Father reciprocates. And his love for this man Jesus not only brings Jesus from death to a new kind of life but brings all those whom Jesus loves to share in that resurrection and new life. So long, of course, as we abide in Jesus's love; so long as we do not value anything else at all more than this love.

But why should Jesus have to go to these extremes? Why does he have to submit to public torture and execution in order to demonstrate and consummate his loving obedience to the Father? Is this some test that the Father has put him to? No. Jesus goes to the extremes which he does because of the *human* world to which he has been sent, the *less* than human world to which he belongs, which is the *only* human world there is. It is because this human world is one of sin (not just a world with sins in it). It is a world maladjusted to the very purpose and point of being human.

The world we have made is one in which what we call 'peace' and 'order' can only be maintained by compromise, by a *moderate* degree of friendship. In this matter Jesus could not compromise, for he bore his mission from the Father. Therefore, to the conscientious administrators who tried to keep a form of peace, or at least tranquillity, in a Roman colony based on exploitation and the fear of violence, and to the priests who wanted to protect the fragile, vulnerable, highly civilized Jewish way of life from the savagery of the barbarian thugs

49

from Rome – to all these people Jesus was an irritation and a nuisance, and liable to cause a breach of the peace. He had to be removed by what we have learned to call a 'surgical strike'.

It was because of the kind of world we have made that Jesus could only ultimately show his love by suffering and death. It is also because of the sort of world we have made that our *abiding* in his love also demands on our part death – not always a public execution, but an acceptance of death. Since our baptism we have all lived under sentence of death: the death of Christ, in which we shall die and so come to resurrection.

This is the good news at one level. But John sees much further into it than that. So he writes of Jesus speaking to his Father of his Father's love for him 'before the foundation of the world' (John 17:24). Jesus, the saint, sharing by grace in the life of God, Jesus growing in sanctity until God's love for him overflows to take in all his sinful friends, so that they are *incorporated* into him, their bodies united with his risen body: all this is just the tip of the iceberg. All this is but the sacrament of a greater reality hidden and revealed within it.

Of course we must not take the 'before' in 'before the foundation of the world' too literally. Without the foundation of the world there could be no before or after. Jesus is speaking of eternity. And, if we think of that as a long time stretching before and after creation, we are simply making a picture – quite a good one, but one by which we must not be misled. It is useful to balance it with another picture: eternity as a depth within time, creation and history: not more in the same dimension, but another dimension. Though remember that that also is only a picture.

The saintliness of Jesus in our history, the whole saving work of Jesus in our history, his human godliness, his grace, is just a sign, a sacrament, of his Godhead in eternity. In eternity Jesus is not just, as we are through him, given a *share* in the Father's life: his life *is* the Father's life. His unity on earth with the Father in obedience is just a pale reflection of the eternal dependence of God the Child, the Word coming forth from and imaging the Father in eternity. In the Godhead the unity that, for us, love and community and friendship aspire to and reach out for, is absolute. 'I and the Father are one' (John 10:30).

We speak of God the Father and God the Son. But their unity is far beyond that of parent and child. The parent brings forth a child like herself, of the same human nature as herself and resembling herself. But, evidently, they are not *one*. They are two separate individuals of the same kind; they are two people; two distinct centres of consciousness, each with their own understanding, their own will, their own point of view. Although we speak of Father and Son as two 'Persons' we certainly do not mean two people. In the Godhead there is but one understanding and one will. There are not different centres of consciousness, different subjects with their own lives to lead. The understanding of God, the will of God, the life of God, are all the one mystery which just is God. Those who love *seek* to be *of* one mind and one heart. The Father and the Son *are* quite simply one mind and one heart.

Jesus, the Word made flesh and dwelling amongst us, is of course a distinct individual, a separate person in our modern sense of the word, a distinct centre of consciousness, with his own will distinct from the will of God, a will that needs to grow in conformity to the will of God. 'My Father, if it is possible, let this cup pass from me; yet not what I want, but what you want' (Matthew 26:39). But God the Son, coming forth in eternity from the Father, is not a different person in that sense.

God the Son is the Word, the concept, coming forth from God in his eternal contemplation of the divine life – as the Holy Spirit, coming forth from the Father through the Son, is his eternal delight in contemplating that divine life. This eternal word, and this eternal joy, go together. Where the Word is, there is the Spirit. And that is why, in living out the sacrament of this eternal life, Jesus says to his faithful disciples: 'I have said these things to you so that my joy may be in you, and that your joy may be complete' (John 15:11). The joy

Jesus refers to here is not just the human reassurance, that all things will be well, that the suffering and death of Christ will be life-giving for the whole world, a joy in the fulfilment of God's loving design for humankind, the joy that comes from hearing the word of the gospel. No, not just that: this joy is the eternal joy which is the Holy Spirit, the joy that God has; not just his joy in loving us, but the joy he has in *being God*. That's what we share.

So, at its greatest depth, the *word* we receive is not just the good news of our liberation, our salvation; it is not just the forgiveness of our sins; it is the *eternal* Word that was in the beginning with God, the Word that was God. And the *joy* that we are given is not just the joy of release from bondage, from evil, the end of the world of violence and domination and killing. It is the incomprehensible mystery of the joy of *God* in being God that was before the foundation of the world.

When the eternal Word of God is fully spoken in our world (and, as I have said, that had to mean the cross), when that Word is heard throughout the world, then the eternal joy bursts out in all the world; the Holy Spirit of God's delight is poured out. And that is why the final feast in our celebration of our salvation, our release from slavery to sin through the cross of Christ, will be the feast of our divinity, our beginning to live the eternal life of the Trinity: the feast of Pentecost.

Chapter 8

Poverty and God

A man ran up and knelt before him, and asked him, 'Good Teacher, what must I do to inherit eternal life?' ... Jesus, looking at him, loved him and said, 'You lack one thing; go, sell what you own, and give the money to the poor, and you will have treasure in heaven; then come, follow me.' When he heard this [the man] was shocked and went away grieving, for he had many possessions.

(Mark 10:17–22)

I thought we might reflect for a minute or two on the connection Jesus makes between possessions and sorrow. The story quoted above comes from Mark. But Luke has it as well (Luke 17:18–25). And he also has the converse proposition: 'Blessed are you who are poor' (Luke 6:20). Jesus, of course, makes a lot of wild statements, but he seems especially emphatic about this one. There is something wrong with being rich and something right with being poor. The last bit, of course, seems not only wild but obscene. Anyone who can think that, for example, starving children or slum-dwellers are fortunate or blessed or happy has to have a twisted mind.

Yet Jesus also tells us that unless we feed people who are hungry, find somewhere to live for the homeless and clothes for those who need them, and unless we care for people in need, then (like most of the rich) we shall not enter the kingdom. So when Jesus says, 'Blessed are you who are poor', he is not recommending complacency in the face of cruelty and injustice, or in the face of any human suffering. So, what is so good about poverty and what is so bad about riches?

I want to suggest that there is something godlike about being able to live in poverty; so we shall have to think about the poverty of God. And I also want to suggest that there is something less than human about needing to live with riches. And the movement from riches to poverty, from having to not having, can be a movement not only to being more *human* but to being *divine*. In a way, the success story for Christians is from riches to rags. Of course, it is a *story* I am speaking about, and that means *movement* in a certain direction; for human being is human becoming. Riches and poverty in themselves represent two extremes, two directions we might aim at. Riches represent the ideal of taking the world for your own use; poverty represents the ideal of complete freedom from possessions. Whichever we aim at we could never attain for ourselves. But poverty we can in the end be given. Sometimes we think of that as death, the cross, and sometimes as resurrection, new life.

I would like to contrast *possessions* and *being*. We *take* possession of things. Even if they are gifts we can either *take* them or refuse them. *Taking* is essential to possessions. Being or life, on the other hand, cannot, in this sense, be *taken*. It can only be sheer gift.

No one can take upon herself life; nothing can bring itself into existence. Always we receive being from another or from others. To aim at riches is to aim at taking possession of things, even, perhaps, taking possession of people. To aim at poverty is to aim at the giving of life, and this comes from gratitude for receiving life ourselves. And giving life is a specially godlike activity.

It is simply not possible for God to be like someone who aims at riches. We cannot speak literally of the riches of God, for he has not, and could not have, any possessions. It is true that often enough, in the psalms for example, we speak of God as though he were landlord of the whole earth: 'In his hand are the depths of the earth; the heights of the mountains are his also; The sea is his, for he made it, and the dry land, which his hands have formed' (Psalm 95:4–5). But these are *images* to be offset by other images, just like the images of God as a warrior or a rock or an eagle. We have, and we need to have, hundreds of images of God, incompatible with each other and not to be forced into some system, not to be taken literally. The image of God as a wealthy landowner holding court amongst his tenants is one of these. We cannot speak literally of the riches and possessions of God for he *could not* take anything to use for his own purposes. He can only use one creature for the sake of another, for the benefit of another. Nothing is or acts for the benefit of God.

We cannot speak literally of the riches of God. But I think we can speak literally of the poverty of God. Of course, his poverty is not the same as our poverty, as his wisdom is not the same as ours. But he is literally poor because he simply and literally has no possessions. He takes nothing for his own use. He only has life and being. And, if you want to press the point, he does not even *have* life, as he does not *have* wisdom or *have* goodness. In God, being alive or being wise or being good are just simply being God and nothing more, nothing extra he *has*. So for us to aim at poverty is for us to aim in the direction of the simplicity and poverty of God – a direction away from possessing to being.

God's creative act is an act of God's poverty, for God gains nothing by it. God makes without becoming richer. His act of creation is purely and simply for the benefit of his creatures. We are sometimes tempted to ask what motive God had for making the world – meaning 'What did he hope to gain by it?' But, of course, this question is absurd. It is only creation that gains by God's act. It is a purely gratuitous act of love, that characteristic act of love which is the giving of life.

The beauty of creation adds nothing to the beauty of God, as the light of the moon adds nothing to the light of the sun but simply reflects it. And God's delight in his creatures and their beauty is not something extra to his delight in the beauty of his creative divinity itself – the delight that we call the Holy Spirit. For the Holy Spirit is just God's delight in his own life as he contemplates it in conceiving his Word. Or, as we say more formally, the Spirit proceeds from the Father through the Word. This eternal delight is the *joy* that belongs to aiming at poverty, as *sorrow* belongs to possessions.

We can aim at riches. We can think of human living as a matter of taking possession of more things. Or we can aim at poverty: we can think of human living as a matter of growing up in our being. The one who aims at poverty knows that we can only live by throwing ourselves away. 'Those who try to make their life secure will lose it, but those who lose their life will keep it' (Luke 17:33).

We do not live by building ever more secure fences of possessions around ourselves, but by giving to others space to live. This is to give life to others. The human animal, human society, flourishes, not to the extent that it possesses riches, but to the extent that we give life to each other, to the extent that we imitate the creativity of God. Of course, as creatures we can only imitate it from a distance. We cannot act, as God does, for *no* benefit to ourselves. But we can live (either more or less) by the free gift we make to others. It is a question of which direction we are aiming for.

All this is just the platitude that the human animal lives by friendship and that human society perishes without it. But to aim at riches is to go away sorrowful because they are, in the end, corrosive of friendship. To aim at poverty, on the other hand, is to build friendship. And to aim at poverty, to grow up by living in friendship, is to imitate the life-giving poverty of God, to be godlike. The gospel does not tell us to have no possessions. It tells us to *aim* at poverty, to move towards it, and certainly not to aim at *riches*. We cannot serve both God and riches. There is something bizarre about the present popularity of the word 'market' as a metaphor for human society. Markets are surely a good and necessary part of living together, as are law courts and lavatories. But none of these are a useful model for what human society essentially is. Personal friendship *is* such a model. I am not saying that society should consist of nothing but personal friendships, for there is a greater friendship that belongs to a community as a whole, and a yet greater friendship that belongs to our community in Christ. But personal friendship is an illuminating image or metaphor for a human living which would be an imitation or reflection of God's creative poverty. The cares and insecurity of Mark's rich man sent him away in sorrow. By contrast, to aim at poverty is to be given the joy by which we live in the Spirit – not only in this life but in eternity.

Chapter 9

Possession and Forgiveness

People who have been horribly treated by others, people who have been tortured, and especially people who have been abused in childhood, sometimes suffer from a strange condition called 'multiple personality'. It seems that these people are, at different times, quite distinct individuals who do not even know each other. It is as though there were one or more strangers inside them, strangers with alien and often horrifying behaviour. In the famous story, Dr Jekyll is haunted in this way by the murderous Mr Hyde.

Psychologists now recognize that multiple personality sometimes comes from people not being able to face up to terrible parts of their life-stories, terrible parts of themselves. The memory of suffering that was not just pain but pain deliberately inflicted by another human being is simply unbearable – especially as it goes with irrational but awful feelings of guilt. People suppress such memory from their consciousness so that part of themselves lives on isolated in the dark part of their minds which they dare not enter. And from time to time it emerges and takes over.

This, I think, is what in the world of Jesus was called 'being possessed by devils'. It was understood that those so possessed were not sinners. Yet they were living and horrific pictures of what sin means. Those possessed had been shattered by an experience of the total breakdown of love. They were victims of the work of the devil. So, in Mark's gospel, for instance, the work of Jesus is shown particularly clearly in the casting-out of devils, in restoring broken people to wholeness. When Jesus encounters people tormented and torn apart by guilt and self-disgust, they recognize that he loves them. And they recognize that he loves not just the nice, respectable and grateful parts of them, but the shamefulness and the darkness as well as the light. What had been demonic, because it had a cancerous life of its own within them, is cast out, not by dividing it from them, but by bringing it within their acceptance.

It is undoubtedly good to try to be cheerful in your own pain and sickness. It is right not to whine and rail uselessly against it, but to make whatever good can be made of it by patience and courage. Nevertheless, it is striking that Jesus never talks about sickness as something to be tolerated. For him, it is just the work of his enemy, and it angers him. He is insistent (as with the man born blind in John 9) that the victim is not a sinner. He firmly states that sickness is the visible sign of the devil's hatred of all that is human, the visibility of what John calls 'the sin of the world' (John 1:29), and the visibility of what he refers to as the power of 'the ruler of this world' (John 12:31; 14:30; 16:11).

Of all sickness, demonic possession is the clearest sign of the power of evil. And, like all works of evil, it is founded in fear. People possessed are profoundly afraid of a part of themselves – so afraid that they cannot bear to admit that it exists. They are pictures (but just pictures) of true sinners: the self-righteous, who cannot bear to admit to their own sin because they are sure that if they did they would not be loved, even by themselves. True sinners have to believe in themselves (or try to) because they do not believe in God's love. They think that they can only be loved if they deceive themselves and others.

The only remedy for this is the conviction, the faith, that comes to us in Jesus: that God is a love which loves us even when we are sinners.

We are quite naturally prone to say that God is angry with us when we sin. And, of course, the Bible speaks frequently of the wrath of God – wrath especially against those who oppress and exploit his particular friends: the poor and unprotected; the widow and the orphan. And this is a perfectly good way of talking. But the language is figurative. It makes an image of God. There is nothing wrong with such imagery as long as we do not let it confuse us into thinking that it represents the last word on God. As St Thomas Aquinas tells us (*Summa Theologiae* Ia, 1,9), we need a lot of images for God. In particular, we need conflicting, incompatible and grotesque ones. The more images we have, says Thomas, the less likely we are to *identify them* with God and the more likely we are to realize that God is the incomprehensible mystery behind all images. So there is nothing wrong with thinking of God as angry about our sin. Yet it would be wrong to think that this is the end of the matter. We have to set images of God's anger beside images of God as constantly tolerant and compassionate. We have to set them beside images of God as forgetting our offences and so on. If we work simply with idols and images, we are liable to tell a story like this: first I sin and God is angry; then I repent and beg for forgiveness; and, after a while, God relents and forgives me and is pleased with me again. And this is perfectly in order considered as a story. But it is not the literal truth.

The literal truth is that when God forgives us he doesn't change his mind about us. Out of his unconditional, unchanging, eternal love for us he changes our minds about him. It is God's loving gift that we begin to think of repenting for our sin and of asking for his mercy. And that repentance does not *earn* his forgiveness. It *is* his forgiveness under another name. The gift, the grace, of contrition just is God's forgiveness. The gift of contrition is, for example, the grace we celebrate in the sacrament of penance. If we go to confession, it is not to plead for forgiveness from God. It is to thank him for it. The gift of contrition is the gift of recognizing God's unswerving love for us. It is the gift of having the confidence to confess our sins, to admit the truth. And if we do that, then, as Jesus told us, the truth will set us free (cf. John 8:32).

When we have been given this faith in a love which brushes aside our wickedness and accepts us although we are sinners, then we are released, then we are forgiven, then we are ready to love in our turn. We are not forgiven and healed because we repent. We repent because God shows us his love in forgiving and healing us. We confess our sins because we are free to do so, free from the desperate need to justify ourselves and prove ourselves right, free from fear of ourselves. And, in the freedom which comes from the Spirit of God's love making us children of God, we are free to pass on that Spirit of love and forgiveness to each other.

Chapter 10

Sin

Let's think about sin.

First of all, sin is something we know about by faith. Without our faith we would not know about it. For sin is about being out of friendship with God. And it is only from the preaching of the Bible in the Church that we know anything about being given friendship with God. Anybody might work out, just by contemplating the world and thinking about it, that it had to be *created* and kept in being by what we call 'God', a mystery beyond the whole universe whom we do not understand. But that God loves his human creatures so much that he wants them to be, not only happy, flourishing, fulfilled human beings, but living in his friendship, sharing his own divine life: this is something we would never have known if God had not revealed it to us – first to the Jews of old, and then, in Christ Jesus, to the whole of humankind.

You don't need God to reveal it to you that there are ways of eating and drinking and generally conducting your life that will keep you healthy. And you don't need God to reveal it to you that there are other ways that will be bad for you. You learn these things from traditions of human knowledge and from your own experience. In the same way, you don't need God's revelation to tell you that there are ways of living with others, ways of behaving, that will encourage friendship, a peaceful, harmonious society, and a reasonably flourishing human life: ways of living that will enable you to grow out of being infantile, greedy, selfish and aggressive into a mature person that people enjoy having about the place. And you don't need God's revelation to tell you that there are ways of living that have just the opposite effect. You don't need the Bible to tell you that.

We can get a certain distance with these matters, if we work at it, without even having heard about our *true* destiny, which is not just to have a human life as civilized and reasonable as possible, but to have an eternal divine human life. The Bible tells us that we can and must go far beyond being successfully *human* beings. We are called, all of us, to be *divine* human beings, human beings who share the life and friendship of our creator. The Bible also tells us that this enormous leap from simply being human to entering the Godhead is not something we have to work at at all. God does it all for us because he is in love with us. It is a present to us, the only authentic Christmas present: the present which, in fact, is Christmas. Now sin means spurning this gift because we want something else more. It seems incredible that anyone would do that. It isn't as though it were difficult to accept this free gift of divinity, as it *is* difficult to learn how to be an honest or unselfish or chaste or patient person. The reason why people can prefer something else to God's gift of himself is that it is not easy to recognize the gift, and sometimes we would rather not. We know about it only in the darkness of faith. We have to take God's Word for it. We can *see* riches and comfort and a life of security and ease: they are obviously attractive, and they attract us. But the gift of God comes to us as a power: the 'power of the Holy Spirit'. And it is the power to love each other with the love that God has for us, the power to give ourselves away to others. And the use of this power can easily conflict with the obvious attractions of lesser goods. Possessions and security and ease are obviously good; but sometimes we may only seek them at the expense of charity, of the power of loving that God offers to us. And, though accepting the gift of charity may not be hard work, it is risky, dangerous and frightening. Remember what happened to Jesus, who was the Word, the expression of God's love amongst us.

St Thomas Aquinas said that there is a certain order of priorities in charity (*Summa Theologiae* 2a2ae, 25,12). This is love, John says (1 John 4:10): 'not that we loved God but that he loved us and sent his Son'. Because of this, says Aquinas, we should first of all love God; and secondly we should love *ourselves* – and this means that we should want the greatest good for ourselves: to live the divine life, to share in God's life. Thirdly, we should love our *neighbour*. But we cannot do that unless we love God and ourselves in charity, for to love our neighbours in charity is to love them because God does. We love our neighbours not, first of all, because of what we see in them, but because of what God sees in them. They are, as Paul said, those 'for whom Christ died' (cf. Romans 5:8), those for whom God died. And if we see them in that light, we shall also see much more in them than we would if we just started with 'What do *I* see in them?' Fourthly, says Aquinas, we are to love our own bodily lives. We are to enjoy living because it is God's gift to us. We are to be passionately delighted by life, to be grateful for it and live it to the full, provided that we do not set it above love of our neighbour, of ourselves, or of God.

But, all the same, it is dangerous and frightening to live in charity. If we live as Christ did, we are in danger of dying as Christ did. And why is this? Many centuries ago, highly intelligent and sophisticated Jews meditated on this problem, which you might call the inherent maladjustment of man: why is the human animal the wildest and most dangerous on the face of the earth? They came to the conclusion that there was just one choice before human animals. They had to either accept or reject what they called the righteousness of God, the righteousness which is God, the divine life. That is the theology behind the story of the Garden of Eden. There was no way that human beings could be simply human. They had to be either superhuman or inhuman. They either had to live by the Torah, by loving each other as God loves us, or else by violence, terror and oppression, by the strong exploiting the weak. We have made our choice, and the world we have made is one based on fear, driven by fear of poverty, starvation, prison, torture and killing. This is what, in John's gospel, Jesus calls 'the World'. This is what we are born into. This is what we are enmeshed in. And the reason why it is dangerous and frightening to try to live by charity is that the World is likely to hate you if you do. Charity represents a threat to the structures of power and domination by which the World is kept in a kind of stability. This is the *first* and fundamental meaning of sin: the sin of the world, the sin that is built into the world in which we have our origin. When we speak of 'original sin' we are not referring to some ancient and original sin of our first parents – though, of course, we do have and cherish a profound story about first parents, a story designed to say that God did not make us maladjusted, that evil, sin and unhappiness came into the world through human beings and not by God's plan. But when we speak of original sin we mean the sin we have from our own origin in this world: not a sin we have committed, but a distortion of our world which leads us away from God, a distortion that leads us, when we encounter love, to crucify it.

But the gospel, the good news, is that just as man brought evil into the world, so it was a man who saved the world (cf. Romans 5:12 *et seq.*). The love of the human being Jesus Christ for his Father, his obedience and faithfulness to his mission, which was simply the mission of being human, being the first really human being, and which led him to his judicial murder by the colonial power, this love and obedience earned for *him* his conquest of death and, for his brothers and sisters, their rescue from sin and death. This man was indeed the eternal Son of the Father; yet we are not saved immediately by that. We are saved by his human sanctity, the grace by which he was wholly obedient to his Father in heaven. We are born into the world of sin, a world of greed, cruelty and selfishness. But by our faith, by our baptism, which is the sacrament of faith, we renounce our citizenship in this world and are dedicated to the world of the future, the world of peace and justice and love.

Yet though because of the strong obedience of Jesus of Nazareth we are no longer subject to the Prince of this world, the World remains our enemy, seeking to make us conform to the ruined empire of sin. And sometimes, by neglect of the grace we are offered in Christ, we are seduced and behave as citizens of this world. But Christ is always waiting and anxious to bring us back to him, to give us the grace of contrition, which is the forgiveness of our sin. This is the *second* meaning of sin: not now the sin of the World, the pervasive structure of sin into which we were born, but our own personal betrayal of our baptism, a serious attack upon the life of charity, a going over to the side of the enemy, of the establishment. Because we have opted for the empire of death that is doomed to destruction, and because we have been unfaithful to the world of the future life, we call this sin 'mortal' or 'fatal' sin. It is mortal in that we reject the life of charity, the life of God within us. And, just as if we had killed ourselves, we have no way of coming back to life. Only the absolutely unmerited gift of grace, of contrition, can bring us back to divine life again.

But much more common than this, and what we ordinarily think of as sins, are sins in a *third* and utterly different sense. These are what have come to be called 'venial' sins. And they do not destroy, or even diminish, the divine life of charity within us. Aquinas, most encouragingly, says that it is not possible for the life of charity within us to be diminished by any action of ours since the life of charity is the work of God (cf. *Summa Theologiae* 2a2ae, 24,11). We can lose it altogether by real, serious, mortal sin. But that is all. Sin, in this third sense, is simply failing to grow in charity, missing the opportunities of growth. And its remedy is simply trying to be a bit more caring and loving towards those we live amongst.

Chapter 11

Self-Love

'You shall love the Lord your God with all your heart, and
with all your soul, and with all your mind.' This is the greatest
and first commandment. And a second is like it: 'You shall love
your neighbour as yourself.'

(Matthew 22:37–40)

When we read this passage we are inclined to think: here are
two commandments, one about loving God, and the other
about loving our neighbour. We are inclined to think that it
sets before us two objects for our love: God and neighbour.
Some people would say that these two commandments are
really one: that you love God by loving your neighbour. But if
you read the passage carefully, you will see that it is indeed
about two commandments.

Yet it is not about having two objects of love. Nor is it about
having one object for our love. It is about having three. And, in
some ways, the third one, which we can easily fail to notice, is
the key one. In one way, it is where we start from: loving
ourselves. I don't mean that it is more important to love
ourselves than to love God. I just mean that loving yourself is
the way you love God. I mean that loving yourself is, in a way,
more important than loving your neighbour because, without
loving yourself, it is quite impossible to love your neighbour. As
Aquinas says, we should first love God, then ourselves, then our
neighbour, then our bodily life (*Summa Theologiae* 2a2ae, 25,12).

If you ask yourself, 'What does it really *mean* to love God?', the chances are that your mind will go quite blank. Of course you can evade the question, as so many moralists do, by quoting St John: 'If you love me, you will keep my commandments' (John 14:15). You may say that loving God consists in doing what he tells us. But it doesn't. It is possible, for a while anyway, to behave in accordance with many excellent commandments without loving God at all or without even believing in God. And anyway, here is Jesus telling us that the first commandment itself is to love God.

So what does loving God itself consist in? I think we can best get at this by asking what it means to love ourselves. And we can best get at what it means to love ourselves if we first of all see what it is like *not* to love oneself.

The root of all sin is fear, a fear which is a disbelief in oneself, the fear that really, in oneself, one does not matter, does not really exist – the fear that if one really looked into the centre of oneself, there would be nothing there: the fear not just that one is playing a false part, wearing a disguise, but that one is nothing *but* the disguise. It is this fear that gives rise to the desperate attempt to put something there, to make something of ourselves, or the desperate fight to prevent others making nothing of us by taking away the masks. And so we make ourselves somebody through power over others and through possessions, which are a sort of power. Or we sink into some distracting pleasure so that we can forget the emptiness. And, of course, we hate those who threaten our self-flattering images. And all this is rooted in fear, because we cannot believe in ourselves, because we cannot believe that we matter just because we are ourselves. It is rooted in the fact that we cannot love ourselves.

Self-love, delight in being yourself, is the very opposite of smugness and complacency. Smugness is satisfaction in what you have or what you have done instead of in yourself. Smugness is a bit like valuing something simply for its price, for what it will fetch, instead of in itself. Remember Oscar Wilde's remark about the man who knew the price of everything and the value of nothing. The Pharisee who said, 'God, I thank you that I am not like other people' (Luke 18) was being smug. He was loving not himself but his achievements. And, of course, the other face of smugness is anxiety and depression – the worry that one's price is not high enough, the worry that one does not matter. These two afflictions are also called presumption and despair. They are the same thing really.

Philosophers have talked about how important it is to know oneself; and they are quite right. But Christianity is a wisdom concerned with how to love oneself, and how to rejoice in being.

You learn to love yourself by recognizing that you are loved. That is clear enough at all sorts of levels. It is the most elementary truth of education that children learn to accept themselves, to be secure, to love and value themselves, through knowing that they are accepted and valued and loved. And when Christians talk of God they are just talking of the fact that we are *ultimately* loved, that even if all other love should fail us there is a fundamental love through which we are. Christian faith is the belief that we matter because we are loved by God.

The root of the whole thing is faith. As fear is the root of sin, faith is the root of love. It is our faith that God loves us that makes us able to love ourselves and, through that, to be grateful for the gift of ourselves. And this gratitude for *being* is the first thing we mean by loving God.

Of course loving God is not confined to being grateful for the gift of ourselves. To love God is also to be grateful for the gift of the whole universe and, above all, for the gift of others. And this is to love our neighbour. But until you love yourself, and are grateful for yourself, you do not see the universe for what it is. Your vision is tainted and distorted by the questions 'What's in it for me?' 'How can I use the world to give me status, to hide the emptiness within?'

It is only if you love yourself because you take yourself as a gift from God, because you see yourself as given, granted, by God, that you can 'take yourself for granted'. And then you can see others and other things in their own right and not just as part of your plans, as material to be manipulated. And this is the beginning of love.

Let's think a bit more about gratitude and gifts. To be grateful for a gift is not just to value it, to find it good. It is also to see it and treat it as an expression of the value and goodness of the giver. The words 'thank' and 'think' come from the same root. To say 'thank you' is to say 'I *think* of you in this gift; I see it as also a gift of yourself to me, as a communication of yourself to me.'

Of course there is a lot of difference between seeing yourself as a gift from God and seeing other things as gifts. And there is one most important one. If someone gives you, let us say, a bottle of excellent wine, there are separate ways in which you could value it. You could value it for its price, for what it would fetch if you sold it. You could also value it precisely as a gift, as coming from the giver, as an expression of his or her love and friendship. Now the curious and mysterious thing about your self, the thing that makes you different from a bottle of wine (and, after all, one isn't simply a wine-container) is this: you can value and enjoy the wine just for its own excellence, for its own sake, without considering either its price or who gave it to you. But if you try to value your self, your being, for its own sake, you will find that you always slip into one of the other two ways of valuing. You will find that you are being smug and self-satisfied and valuing yourself for your possessions and achievements, which is like valuing the wine for its price. Or you will find that you are valuing yourself as a gift from God, as an expression of his love. There isn't any middle way. It doesn't seem possible to value yourself for what you are in yourself regardless of who *gave* you.

In fact you are really rather more like a letter than a bottle of wine. Suppose that I happen to know a famous poet or novelist who writes me a letter with news about his family and what he is doing (the poem or novel he is working at). When I get the letter one thing I could think is how I could one day sell it so as to make money. I hope this would not be my first thought. I hope I would value the letter for what it is in itself. But when I do that I am immediately seeing it as coming from my friend. To value the letter for its own sake is to be grateful for it, to say 'thank you', to think of my friend through it. Thinking of a bottle of wine as a gift is different from thinking of it in itself, but thinking of a letter as a gift is the same as thinking of it in itself.

Now it is this way with ourselves. To see ourselves as gift from God is just to look deeply into ourselves, to see ourselves for what we really are. You cannot love yourself, your real self (as distinct from valuing your price or what you will fetch) without being grateful to God, without thanking him, thinking him through yourself. And it is only when you do this, when you thank God for yourself, for the gift of existence, that you are released from the prison of self-seeking to value others for their own sake, which is to value them too as gifts of God. That is why Jesus tells us to love our neighbour as ourselves. He is asking us to love our neighbour in the way we love ourselves – in gratitude to God.

But there is much more to it than this. For when you do it, when you actually thank God for your being and for others (not just when you *think* about it but when you *do* it), you discover a further truth: that the thing you are most grateful for, the greatest gift of God, is the gratitude itself. The greatest gift of God to you is not just that he made you, but that you love him. The greatest gift of God to you is that you can speak with him and say 'thank you' to him as to a friend – that you are on intimate speaking terms with God. God has made us not just his creatures but his lovers; he has given us not just our existence, our life, but a share in *his* life. We converse familiarly with God on equal terms as the Son does with the Father. We love God with the same love that Jesus had for him, the love we call the Holy Spirit. And we love ourselves not only because

73

we came forth from God but because our life is God's life, the life of the Spirit. And our love for our neighbour is this same Spirit. That means that whatever you do from love for anyone is not just a sign of human goodness, not just a sign of the goodness God has given you, but a manifestation of God. In our everyday routine acts of friendship, forbearance, forgiveness, we reveal the eternal love of God to the world. We bring the world to the presence of God. And we do this because we love ourselves as gift of God, as filled with the Holy Spirit, the eternal life of God. And this life is one which we shall have and enjoy in eternity, when all the masks have perished and there is no more striving for importance, achievements, or even for goodness. This life is one in which we shall live as God himself lives in the eternal exchange of love.

Chapter 12

Ash Wednesday

Those of you who are lucky enough to have read Flan O'Brien's *The Third Policeman* will remember De Selby's reflections on mirrors. He points out that when you look in a mirror you do not see yourself as you are. Because of the finite speed of light you see yourself just a fraction of a second younger than you now are. He suggests that with a series of mirrors you could see yourself as younger and younger, going back to childhood.

I remind you of this with a view to Ash Wednesday, on which Christians enter the season traditionally associated with self-denial. And, when thinking about all that, it is worth pausing to look at what we mean by 'self' and 'denial'. The point of Flan O'Brien's joke is that the self I look at is no longer me. I am not to be found in what is looked at, but in the looking; to live, to be alive, to be myself is to be going *beyond* the self I have, the self I possess, the self I look at as mine. This is what Jesus said: Only the one who loses his self will save it (cf. Matthew 10:39 and Luke 9:24). He wasn't just talking about martyrdom or his own death, though this is the ultimate expression of the truth. He was talking about what it is to be a human being: always to be going beyond a self which has become a possession, a property, something to be proud of.

It isn't just a question of feeling guilty about what we are like. Long before we are *ashamed* of ourselves, we should be *amused* at ourselves – at our self-importance and self-conceit. But, of course, the world being what it is, that self-importance, which at first is merely ridiculous, soon leads to things that are shameful: to selfishness and cruelty and greed.

So there are two kinds of reason for self-denial. First, that the self is not something we should possess and cling to anyway; self-assertion is a failure to take the risks of living; it is settling for what we were, for the image in the mirror. And, secondly, that the self we had was pretty bad anyway. The sensible way to look in the mirror is not with satisfaction but with contrition.

All this is true all year, of course. To live is not to be the person in the mirror but the person who is going beyond that, who is looking in the mirror. To refuse to die to the past is to refuse to live. To jib at contrition is to jib at grace and new life. Sorrow for sin is not the opposite of joy; it is a constituent of it.

All this, I say, is true all year. But we have Lent for dramatizing it. In Lent we put it on stage. We symbolize it in order to make it real for us. Observance of Lent is a work of art: it is as when a painter or a poet puts his subject into symbols, not as a substitute for reality but to bring us into the real. This is true of all our liturgical life; but in Lent the play we put on is the play about self-denial, about dying in order to rise again, about losing ourselves in order to find ourselves, about finding holiness in confessing our sins, about finding happiness in being ashamed of ourselves.

Observing Lent, putting on this play is a physical matter. You could no more observe Lent without actual fasting or some kind of bodily inconvenience than you could make a painting without canvas and paint, or a play without some kind of stage and costumes and props. These things have to be really physically there. At the same time, however, their value is not in their own physical reality but in what they symbolize or dramatize. You cannot observe Lent by just thinking about self-denial. You dramatize it by, say, fasting. But the point of fasting is not to deny yourself by starving to death; it is to symbolize all the self-denial that is part of being alive.

Of course, there are all sorts of pitfalls here. Dealing with symbols is always tricky since they can so easily be used for lying as well as for telling the truth. The symbols of self-denial can be used for self-assertion. An actor can ruin a play by showing off on the stage. That's what Jesus is talking about when he says 'Beware of practising your piety before others in order to be seen by them' (Matthew 6:1). And we can show off to ourselves as well. We can be proud of the symbols of our self-denial. We can congratulate ourselves on giving up smoking, or whatever. There's no technique for preventing this happening. My guess is, though, that the less we think up special personal quirky ways of dramatizing our self-denial the less we are likely to be pleased with ourselves. Probably, the more conventional we are the better.

I haven't talked about the other and equally important and traditional side of Lenten observance. If we are to die to ourselves it is because we are to live for others. The other side of fasting is almsgiving, helping those in need. But here, too, remember that we are engaged in a drama, a symbolic act. We do not give alms in Lent because we are under the illusion that almsgiving will solve the problem of world poverty; and by the same token we do not think it foolish to give alms just because we know it will *not* solve that problem. The point is again to dramatize for ourselves the reality of poverty and oppression and need, and of our responsibility in the face of it. Almsgiving is not a substitute for political action. Art is not a substitute for reality.

And so in Lent, by our small practices of self-denial and giving to others, we make a special drama of our ordinary lives, a drama of death and resurrection. And in Holy Week we sum it all up in our representations of the passion of Christ. In the feast of Easter, the feast of our baptism and of the eucharist, our drama, our symbols, merge with the sacramental signs in which symbol and reality become one. In the

Easter sacraments we really do share in the self-abandonment, the sacrificial death of Christ. And, through this, we share in his new life of the resurrection which is the beginning of our life in the Spirit of love for eternity.

Chapter 13

The Wedding Feast at Cana

First of all, the story of the wedding feast at Cana occurs only in John. And in John it is one of just two stories in which the mother of Jesus plays a part. The Cana story is at the beginning of the gospel: 'Jesus did this, the first of his signs, in Cana of Galilee' (John 2:11). The other story is at the end of the gospel, at the crucifixion, when Jesus says 'It is finished', and bows his head and gives up his spirit (John 19:30). Now I think that we only understand the Cana story if we put it beside, and compare and contrast it with the second one. And that is what I would like to do. Notice that in both cases Mary is simply called 'the mother of Jesus'. It may be that John did not know of the stories of the birth and infancy of Jesus in which Matthew and Luke tell us that she is called Mary. But even if he did, he had, I am going to suggest, very good reasons for calling her 'the mother of Jesus'.

'The mother of Jesus was there. Jesus and his disciples had also been invited to the wedding' (John 2:2). Mary is mentioned before Jesus, which seems a little odd. And it certainly has nothing to do with being courteous. We are meant to focus on the special role of the mother of Jesus. The story is about the marriage feast, and the mother and the wine. The marriage feast is to remind us of the messianic banquet mentioned in the Old Testament – when the hitherto virgin Israel (who has, more or less, kept herself from union with the gods of the nations, i.e. from political entanglements with neighbouring pagan countries) is finally to be wedded to her destined husband, who is to be the Lord. It is the banquet celebrating the union of God and humankind. At this banquet, in Cana something has come to an end: the wine has given out. All that is available is water-jars, 'for the Jewish rites of purification', characteristic of the Old Law that in one respect is passing away and in another is being transformed.

Now two things happen: the mother of Jesus appeals to him to do something about all this; and she is snubbed. Jesus says, 'Woman, what concern is that to you and to me? My hour has not yet come' (John 2:4). Throughout John's gospel, the 'hour' of Jesus means just one thing: the cross: John also calls it the 'lifting-up' of Jesus (cf. John 12:32). And, for John, this means both Jesus's lifting-up on the cross (the failure of his mission) and the lifting-up which is the resurrection (the achievement of his mission, when in his death he gave forth his Spirit into the world). The mother of Jesus, ignoring the snub, says to the servants 'Do whatever he tells you.' They fill the jars with water and it becomes a huge abundance of very good wine: 'You have kept the good wine until now. Jesus did this, the first of his signs, in Cana of Galilee, and revealed his glory; and his disciples believed in him' (John 2:11).

But that is what happened at Cana: a miracle, a *sign*; just a miracle, though, like all miracles, it was meant to, and did, bring about the beginning of faith. Still it was only a miracle.

Cana is a joyful story, a story prefiguring a liberation and a new life to come, fittingly symbolized by the good wine. And in all this the mother of Jesus is brushed aside. But, as I say, John expects us to set this story alongside a second one at the end of the gospel, a story in which new wine has turned sour and we have only vinegar instead. The story of Jesus in all the gospels is the story of the failure of Jesus. He begins so promisingly. The people, especially the poor, are entranced by his message and by his miracles of healing. But by the end they are howling for his crucifixion. His own intimate friends and disciples have deserted him, and their leader, Peter, has disowned him. And at this point in John the mother of Jesus reappears: Jesus is left with the women, the most disempowered in the culture of the time. This all the gospels witness to. But it is only John who says, 'Standing near the cross of Jesus were his mother, and his mother's sister ... and the disciple whom he loved standing beside her' (John 19:25–6). And, says John, Jesus said to his mother, 'Woman, here is your son' (John 19:26).

'Woman' (Greek: *gyne*) is the same word Jesus is quoted by John as using to address his mother at Cana. But then he had brushed her off. This time, however, he says 'behold *your* son'. And this is the central meaning of both the stories. What Jesus did at Cana was only a miracle. And, like all true miracles, it was done by divine power. And with this his mother had nothing to do. It was because he is the son of *God* from eternity that he could work such triumphal wonders. But the human race is not saved by the miracles that Jesus worked. It is saved by his *defeat*, his failure, his acceptance of the cross. The mission that Jesus knew himself to have from his Father in heaven was the mission to be fully human, to be loving and so to be vulnerable, to be able to suffer and die. Jesus was the first completely human person because he lived and died by love, by throwing himself away for the sake of his fellow human beings, even, and most strikingly, for the sake of those who had no love for him. Of course, as with every human being, his humanity could only be perfected by God's grace. But by God's grace this man saved us by loving obedience to his Father's command to be human. And by this obedience, even unto death, in contrast, as Paul says, to the *dis*obedience of Adam (cf. Romans 5), he earned for himself the grace to conquer death and rise from the tomb. And, overflowing from this by the same grace, he earned for his sisters and brothers to join him in his resurrection.

Now all this was made possible, not because Jesus was eternally son of God but because he was son of a woman. That is what he means by 'Woman, here is your son.' When it was only a miracle, only the first *sign* that he was going to perform,

Mary had no part to play except to tell the servants to listen to him and to do what he told them. 'My hour has not yet come.' But now his hour *has* come. And Mary has everything to do with him. For she gave him not his divinity but his humanity. 'Woman, here is your son.' As I see it, we miss the whole point of what John is teaching us if we suppose that Jesus is here speaking of the beloved disciple. He is talking of himself. Only *then* does he say to the disciple: 'Here is your mother' (John 19:27).

Whoever we are to identify the 'beloved disciple' with, it seems fairly clear that he is there to represent the Gentiles – that is, us. He is present by the cross with the mother of Jesus, and Jesus in his dying words makes her the mother of the Church which is now both Jewish and Gentile. Matthew and Luke make the mother of Jesus the fulfilment of the prophesy of the virgin Israel, the one who by the power of the Spirit of God brings forth the saviour. John makes her the representation of the future, the virgin Mother Church from whose womb, as we say at the Easter Vigil, we have been reborn by our baptism: reborn to receive the new life of the Spirit which comes to us from the cross, the Spirit who is the Lord and giver of life, the life of love in which we shall live in eternity.

Chapter 14

Washing and Eucharist

> And during supper Jesus, knowing that the Father had given
> all things into his hands, and that he had come from God and
> was going to God, got up from the table, took off his outer robe,
> and tied a towel around himself. Then he poured water into a
> basin and began to wash the disciples' feet ...
>
> (John 13:3–4)

When Jesus washed the feet of his disciples, he was doing two
things. First of all, he was expressing hospitality: these men are
his guests; he invites them to share in what he has. When you
invited people to eat and drink with you in Jesus's society, the
first thing you did for them as they entered was to arrange for
their feet to be washed. They would be hot and dusty from the
journey. So in washing the feet of his disciples Jesus invites his
followers to be his guests. But Jesus does not just arrange for his
guests to have their feet washed (in the ordinary way you had
a slave to do that). Jesus is both host and slave. He washed the
feet of his own guests. And this takes any possible sting out of
his hospitality. A host is lord of his table. It is he who provides
the food and drink. And his guests, in courtesy, must defer to
him. But Jesus proposes a new kind of hospitality, one in which
the host is also slave and, therefore, not lord; in which the slave
is also host and therefore not subservient. Here is something
that is neither lordship nor servitude. Here is the meal of
equals.

This washing of the feet by the one who is both lord of the

feast and servant is a symbol of a new kind of relationship amongst men and women, a relationship neither of dominance nor subservience but of equality in love, a relationship in which we are equal in love to each other as Jesus and the Father are equal, a relationship in which we are one as he and the Father are one, a relationship which is the Holy Spirit.

St John has his own reasons for leaving it there with the washing of the feet. For him, the Passover marks Christ's crucifixion. It is his time for being lifted up and glorified. The other evangelists (and St Paul) tell us that Jesus celebrated the Passover with his disciples, his friends. And they tell us that, in doing so, he instituted the eucharist. But the story of the eucharistic meal as the synoptic gospels (and St Paul) tell it brings us further into the same mystery that is pointed to in John's account of the washing of the feet: the mystery of our new relationship of brotherhood in Christ.

Let's just look at those words that Jesus said (according to the synoptics and Paul). And, just for a change, let's look at them the other way round. I mean: let us put the emphasis in a different place. Let us read them as saying: 'Jesus took bread and said *this* is my body for you.' Let us read Jesus as saying: 'If you are looking for my body, *this* is it.' 'Body' here certainly doesn't mean something distinct from soul or blood. It just means *Jesus* – his real human being. 'If you are looking for me', he is saying, 'this is where you will find me; this is where you will find my body.' When you have a friend it is his or her bodily presence that matters. It is no (or not much) comfort to know simply that your friend exists if he or she is several hundred miles away. What we desire is bodily presence. But if we seek the bodily presence, the real self, of Jesus for us, where do we find him? Jesus says: don't go looking in the tomb for my body, don't go looking up to heaven for my risen body, don't go looking anywhere, look amongst yourselves, look at the food you eat together, look at the life you share together. This is the kind of thing that my bodily presence is: when you break bread together.

Of course, all breaking of bread together in friendship, in love, is a presence of the body of Christ. When we say grace at meals, when we thank God, make eucharist, we are thanking the Father for the presence of Christ. But the eucharistic meal is special. This meal is the ultimate in meals, the ultimate in sharing food and life together. The Last Supper was, of course, a Passover meal. The bread that Jesus shared with his disciples was unleavened bread. The way to make bread rise, if you don't happen to have any yeast or baking powder, is to mix in a bit of the old fermented leaven from the previous baking – that way all loaves are in continuity with the past. But the unleavened bread is new. It does not depend on the past. It has broken with the past. The meal in which it is broken is the meal of a new community, a new creation. That is why unleavened bread is used in the Passover meal to symbolize the new community of the people of God that was formed at the Exodus. They came out of chaos and darkness and were made into a new people, a new kind of community.

Now Jesus is announcing a new Passover meal and a new people of God. He is announcing the coming of the *Kingdom*. In any meal we have in friendship, in any act of hospitality, any act of sharing life (feeding the hungry, visiting the imprisoned, housing the homeless, celebrating with our friends), we are in the presence of Christ. This is his body. But in our eucharistic meal we are present to each other (and in the presence of Christ) as we *will be* in the Kingdom. We enter for a moment into the world of the future, into that kind of society in which we will simply be the body of Christ, in which there will be no admixture of evil, no alienation. Instead of our friendship being a ray of light amongst the darkness of sin, selfishness, cruelty and domination, as it is now, it will be the whole of our life, all our ways of being together. Into this world we enter for a moment sacramentally in the breaking of the eucharistic bread. When celebrating the eucharist we proclaim that we belong to the kingdom of the future. Or the Kingdom comes and announces that we belong there – a kingdom that is a new community, that gives a new meaning to community, where we break the unleavened bread of sincerity and truth, a kingdom where we find a new relationship between ourselves.

But in the Kingdom we also find a new relationship with God. As our alienation from each other disappears, so does our alienation, our estrangement, from God. God ceases to be in any way an alien, a stranger. He is no longer even a benign stranger looking down on our life.

In the Kingdom, God will no longer be standing over against us either to judge us or to reward us. He will not be the Other, over there or out there or up there. He will be all in all. This is the new covenant with God that we celebrate in the eucharist.

The covenant of the God of the Old Testament with Israel was ratified and celebrated with religious rites, with the blood of animal sacrifices, with special ceremonies set apart from ordinary life. They were set apart because God was set apart. The link with God, the covenant with God, was celebrated in a strange and alien and sacred place with special actions set apart and sacred because God was set apart and sacred. God was a stranger, even though a friendly stranger. Israel was his people. But still he stood over against them and above them.

The new covenant represents a new vision of God. It is not ratified and celebrated with the blood of sacrifice or with any special religious act. It is ratified by what is simply an act of love. An act of love as bloody and horrible as any sacrifice, but first of all simply an act of ordinary love. The new covenant is ratified because Jesus accepted his dreadful death. And he accepted it because he loved us, loved us enough to be close to us, to be close enough to be our victim, close enough to suffer the fate that we impose on love that threatens our world, our world that is based on lies and domination and fear, on anything except love. Jesus died because when we meet love, although we fool ourselves that we will like it, we in fact kill it.

Jesus did not go to Calvary to say mass, to perform any ritual religious act. He was dragged to Calvary because he was prepared to lay down his life for his friends. The blood here is not ritual blood. It is the real blood of a man who was murdered by our police, our soldiers defending our right to live without love. Jesus shed this blood to show that we are his friends, to show that we are friends, in spite of everything, of God.

So this cup that we bless, that we drink and share, is the sign not only of the presence of Jesus, but of Jesus shedding his blood for us, giving his life for us, founding the new covenant of the Kingdom. It is the blood of Jesus whose murder does what all the ritual sacrifices were trying to do. It overcomes the alienation of God which we call sin.

Chapter 15

Easter

Easter seems such a relief after all the austerities of Lent (I hope there were some austerities) and after the grief and dreadfulness of the cross. And we should indeed feel that the cross has been turned into joy. Yet we have to beware of thinking that the cross has been *replaced* by joy: as though while on Good Friday all was gloom and defeat, now it is all different, masterful heaven has intervened, the *deus ex machina* has given us a happy ending after all.

This is the wrong way to put it because Easter is not a cancellation of the cross. It does not, in any important sense, celebrate anything different from the cross. It is the meaning of the cross. Of course, there were two events: a crucifixion and, later, a rising from the dead. But these two events are part of a single story with a single meaning. The resurrection is as inseparable from the crucifixion as the punchline from the rest of the story. Easter is how to look at the cross. It is how faith looks at the cross.

Faith is not, though, a pair of rose-coloured spectacles for looking at the cross – as though we could forget that the cross is an instrument of torture and horror. Faith does not gloss over the cross or reinterpret it by wishful thinking.

Faith, the celebration of Easter, is a looking further into the cross, seeing in and through it to the mystery of love which is what it really is. It is not an alternative to the cross. We have to go through Good Friday to Easter. If we have not come to tears on Friday, we shall miss the mysterious joy of Easter. Seen in faith (that is, seen without our customary distortions and evasions), the cross is the best picture of the resurrection.

What is resurrection? That is: what is the meaning of the cross? In celebrating the eucharist we speak of 'Christ's resurrection and ascension into heaven', and it matters how we punctuate that phrase. We usually say: 'Christ's resurrection [pause] and ascension into heaven'. But it might be illuminating occasionally to say: 'Christ's resurrection and ascension [pause] into heaven', for that brings out more of the truth. The resurrection-and-ascension was all *into heaven*. Christ's resurrection was not just a return to life in this world; it was into heaven, but that does not mean it was life in some kind of 'spirit world'; it was the beginning of a new world, a human bodily life in the Kingdom.

Christ rose from the dead into heaven, into God, so that, as representative of humankind, and first fruits of the redemption, *he* might share the life of God, so that in him *we* should share the life of God.

When St Paul speaks of the resurrection he does not mean that the body of Christ was raised up to join him, to join his 'soul'. His soul is not Christ: as St Thomas Aquinas says: 'My soul is not me.' St Paul means that Christ, the bodily Christ of course (there isn't any other), stops being dead, passes through death, through resurrection, to share the life of God. The man Jesus Christ is not just bodily because of his resurrection. He is alive, he exists, because of his resurrection. The man Jesus Christ only exists by being bodily, by being risen.

The resurrection sets the seal on incarnation: it is not that God was man, but that God *is* man, a human, bodily, animal, alive with the bodily life of God.

Because this man Jesus carried his obedience and love to the point of accepting destruction (not just the torture of the cross, but death, an ending, a total failure), because of this, he has been raised up beyond death to love which is the life of God. The resurrection of Jesus was the creation of the new bodily world, the new way of being human, the new way of being bodily. The risen Jesus did not enter paradise. He *is* paradise. Heaven is not a place beyond the sky. It is the risen Christ, the body of Christ living by love, the beginning of risen humankind, the ultimate future of humanity. It is because our bodies share in this bodily life of Christ (the thing we anticipate and symbolize in the eucharist), it is because we belong to this bodily world, that we conquer death, that we are able to live not for ourselves but by love, the love that Christ brings to us from God. And it is because of this that we celebrate the cross at Easter.

Chapter 16

Resurrection as Epiphany

When he was at the table with them, he took bread, blessed
and broke it, and gave it to them. Then their eyes were opened,
and they recognized him.

(Luke 24:30–31)

I want to talk about recognizing, and the special kind of
recognizing that Luke is talking about here. I think there is a
much deeper meaning in it than appears at first sight.

Suppose you heard that someone you knew fairly well had
died. And suppose that going down the street later you saw
someone who looked familiar; and then looking again you got
a kind of shock – for surely that is Robinson (or whoever) who
died? It would be a startling experience, and you might be so
thrown that you revert to the primitive and almost believe that
what you see is a ghost. And then Robinson (or whoever)
comes over and talks with you. And, of course, he is not a
ghost, 'for a ghost does not have flesh and bones as you see that
I have' (cf. Luke 24:39). So you realize that he is not dead after
all because you have recognized him as the same man.

That would be a very odd experience, one that you would
remember. And it is the framework in which the later
evangelists, Luke and John, put their stories of the appearance
of the risen Christ. What I want to suggest to you, however, is
that this is only a framework: that inside this framework they
have something much deeper and much more important to tell

93

us. The gospel stories, on the surface, are about recognizing a friend whom people thought to be dead. But these are stories designed to tell us who Jesus is. They are aiming to tell us about the divinity of Jesus.

Whenever anyone meets the risen Christ in Luke or John there is a problem about *recognizing* him. The two disciples in Luke's Emmaus story (Luke 24:13–35) do not recognize him until an evening meal which becomes a eucharist. Luke follows this story with another (Luke 24:36–49) in which Jesus appears and the disciples at first take him for a ghost. In John, first Mary Magdalene mistakes him for the gardener (John 20:11–18), then Thomas says he will need to be convinced it really is Jesus by the marks of the nails, and so on (John 20:24–9). Finally, in John 21, Jesus appears by the seashore and none of the disciples dares to ask him, 'Who are you?' (John 21:12).

In all these stories, too, there is a problem about *believing*. At first the witness cannot believe it is Jesus, and then something happens and there is a recognition. This recognition is, in every case, also an act of faith, which should tell us what a very special act of recognition it is. People are not just recognizing Jesus as the man they knew was killed. They are recognizing him as the man they *sort of* knew and *thought* they knew, but didn't *really* know until now.

The appearances of Jesus after his death are not just to show that death did him no harm, that he is back again as good as new, the same Jesus that his friends knew in Galilee. They show us that, of course. But they also tell us much more – or they told the disciples much more. The disciples saw, by faith, and for the first time, *who* this same man Jesus was, who it was that they had been with in Galilee. For Luke and John, the resurrection is a revelation of who Jesus really is. Thomas's reaction is not just: 'It's you; the man I already know, my friend.' It is: 'My Lord and my God' (John 20:28). The whole of John's gospel has been leading up to this revelation of who Jesus is. And it is completed in the resurrection of Jesus. Or, as St Paul says, Jesus was 'declared to be Son of God with power according to the spirit of holiness by resurrection from the dead' (Romans 1:4).

Recognizing somebody, knowing who they are, is in any case a mysterious business. It is not just a matter of knowing what they do, where they come from, how they slot into your world (or it need not be). It can be something much deeper than that. For loving someone is uniquely getting to know *who* they are – not just what they are like, but getting in contact with their real self. You really begin to know someone you love. You begin to recognize them. *Who anyone is* is a kind of mystery, something we enter into when we 'know them personally', as we say. And it is something we never finish exploring.

With Jesus, the mystery of who he is arises even before his resurrection. It is not only the risen Christ who is hard to recognize; even before that, there is the question, 'Who do the crowds say that I am?' (Luke 9:18) It is in the mystery of *who* Jesus is that his divinity lies. You reach it by something akin to the personal love by which you come to know who your beloved is – and not just something akin to this love but, in fact, a deeper exploration going in and through such personal love. This is what we call faith.

Faith is not first of all accepting certain truths about Jesus. It is first of all knowing who he is – which is a truth about him in a very odd sense. Faith is knowing Jesus for who he is.

It is like when you recognize a friend and say, 'It's you of course.' And then you go on to say, 'Do you remember when we met in the pub? I'll never forget how you rescued me from that terrible old bore.' Those memories are rather like the articles of faith or the story in the gospels; we use them to *celebrate* our recognition. We recite the creed out of our exuberance at meeting Jesus again. But the doctrine, the statements of faith, the scriptures, are nothing without the faith, the recognition of who Jesus is that they contain and express.

Let's try to think a little bit more about recognizing by looking at the words 'what', 'which' and 'who'.

You are in a cottage and you hear the sound of mooing. 'What's that?' 'It's a cow.' 'Yes, but which cow?' *What* asks about the sort of thing something is: Felix is a cat; I am human; that is a cow. *Which* asks for identification: which *particular* cat, or human being, or cow? When you thought you saw Robinson in the street, you wanted to identify him, to see if he had the same answer to the '*which* man?' question as did the Robinson you used to know. You were startled to find out that he had. He was identified as Robinson by a '*which* man?' question. And this was remarkable enough: so the man was not dead after all.

But I am saying that the question that mattered for those who met the risen Christ was not 'What is it?', or even just 'Which man is it?', but 'Who is it?' There is a difference, a subtle difference between 'which' and 'who'. And it isn't just that we keep 'who' for human beings. 'Who?' has a different kind of answer from 'Which?' The disciples didn't just want to know whether what they met after the resurrection was really the same Jesus that was crucified (a 'which man?' question). They wanted to know *who* he was anyway.

When you ask *what* something is, you look for information about it, about its nature. When you ask 'which?', you raise a different kind of question, though you are still looking for information of some kind. You identify the particular cow or the particular policeman (if you're lucky) by some distinguishing mark that only she or he has. Usually, for general purposes we identify people by who their parents were, or where they came from. The question 'Which is he?' is not far from the question 'Who's son is he?' But of course the *which* question can be asked about all sorts of things, not just people.

The who question is a 'which man?' or 'which woman?' question with a depth to it. To really know who someone is, is to know which person he or she is. But it is also to know him or her by a direct personal relationship. My beloved is not only identified as the daughter of her parents. She is the one whom I love. This identifies her for me: she is the one I love. *Who she is* is now not exactly information about her; *who she is* is simply herself in herself – not a fact about her but herself.

When I ask '*Which* man is it?' I mean which one instead of which other: is it this one, or that one? But when I ask '*Who?*', at least in this deep sense, I am not sorting out my beloved from other possible candidates. I want to know her just in and for *herself*. I want to know in the deepest sense who she is. To know who she is in this sense is to know *her*, not just *about* her.

And Luke and John are saying that faith in the risen Christ is knowing in this sense who Christ is; it is saying 'My Lord and my God'. For Christ's identity is *recognized* by our faith; it is *established* by the *Father's* love. He is the one God loves.

Way back, centuries ago, they talked at the Council of Chalcedon (451) about Jesus in terms of 'person' and 'natures'. And it was fashionable recently to say that this was because they were all tied up in the language of a particular rather provincial philosophy. And maybe they were. But what they were distinguishing goes straight back to Luke and John. They wanted to isolate the question, 'Who is this?', to see that it is here, and nowhere else, that the divine mystery of Jesus lies. 'Who is Jesus?' or, to put it more graphically, 'Whose son is he?': this is the question that is answered in faith by our response to the Lord. He is indeed identified as the son of David, son of Mary, this says *which* one of us he is. But to answer the deeper question within this question, to say properly who he is, we must say in faith that he is Son of God. In the end Jesus is identified, he is *who* he is, by being the one whom *God* loves: 'This is my Son, the beloved; with him I am well pleased' (Matthew 17:5). And, in Jesus, we share in this love, this identity.

Chapter 17

Ghosts, Burial and Resurrection

While they were talking about this, Jesus himself stood among them and said to them, 'Peace be with you.' They were startled and terrified, and thought that they were seeing a ghost.

(Luke 24:36)

St Luke is not here remarking on the quaint superstitions of the apostles. He is making a very serious point about death and resurrection. We think of people as dying and going to heaven (perhaps by way of purgatory) or else going to hell. And we think, first of all, of both heaven and hell as permanent destinies. Not so the Hebrews, from whose tradition Luke is writing. For them, people had an allotted span of years, a lifetime. And if the Lord was favourable to them, they would live out their whole span of threescore years and ten in peace, and see their children's children to the third and fourth generations. Then they would be gathered to their fathers. The great misfortune was to die young, prematurely, by violence, disease or accident; not to be able to live out your allotted span, not in your proper place on earth but in *sheol* or hell. When you died prematurely, your ghost or shade lived in a disembodied half-life in the underworld, where there was no rejoicing or feasting or praising God, none of the good things of this earth. The Hebrews did not think of this as eternal punishment. The bad thing was that death had invaded your

99

life. It was as though you had a permanent disabling disease. In fact, the Hebrews saw sickness and death or hell as much the same thing. Both were death in life, an attack upon life by death.

So, when you died young, as of course Jesus did, your spirit or ghost was excluded from the joys of life. So the ghost was a sign of death. It was not, as we might imagine, some portion of you that has somehow *survived* death. To be a spirit in this sense, when you ought to be alive, was to be conquered by death. That is why ghosts were (and still are) frightening; they are manifestations of the grave – not of what has survived the grave, but of the grave itself.

It was important to bury a corpse properly, to put it under the earth in the underworld where it belonged, otherwise the restless ghost would be likely to come and seek it out. Now in Luke's story there was some confusion about whether Jesus was properly buried or not. The women had gone to the tomb, but did not find the body. Nor did Peter when he went to look. But if the body were not properly buried, handed over to the underworld, you could expect death to come seeking his victim, his property, in the shape of a ghost.

This is what filled the disciples with alarm and fright. At first, they saw Jesus as a manifestation of death. They have to learn that he is a manifestation of life.

Luke has already told us that the grave of Jesus was empty, that Jesus's corpse was unburied. You might expect death to come as a ghost seeking his spoils. But this is not what happened at all. By his death on the cross, because it was an act of love, Jesus was not conquered by death. On the contrary, he has conquered death. Death has no right to his body. The underworld is *not* the rightful place for the body of Jesus. And that is why the tomb is empty. There is no corpse in the grave. There is the living Jesus, who now asks his disciples to handle and touch him and even to eat with him. The implication is that for those in contact with the body of Jesus, especially those who eat with him (those who belong to his body), there is the same freedom from death. Just as at Emmaus (Luke 24:13–35) it is through eating, through the eucharist, that we share in the resurrection.

But there is more to it than this. As Luke's story continues, Jesus shows his disciples his body by showing them his hands and feet, the place of his wounds. He shows himself as wounded and says 'Have you anything here to eat?' (Luke 24:41). He appears, in fact, as wounded and hungry, just as in Matthew's vision of the judgement: 'I was hungry and you gave me food' (Matthew 25:35).

So the risen Christ appears to us in the eucharist, but also in the wounded, the hungry, in all those who need us. In both cases we can fail to recognize him. The Church with its symbol, the cross, is easy to see as a sign of death; but we know that it is only through the love which accepts death that we can come to real life. In just the same way, the poor, the hungry, the oppressed are easy to see as a sign of death, for so they are. They are, like the Church, like the cross, a threat to life as we know it, to the world as we have built it. It would be easy to shun them and forget them as simply a sign of failure, a sign of death, like a ghost. But Luke is telling us that this is where the risen Lord is. 'Blessed are you who are poor, for yours is the Kingdom of God' (Luke 6:20). It is only by our solidarity with the poor – not a condescending helping hand, but a real identification with them in their suffering and in their struggle – that we belong to the life of the risen Christ and share in his conquest of death.

Chapter 18

Prayer

God became angry with the people of Nineveh. But they repented and 'the people of Nineveh believed God'. And their king issued a decree telling them to obey God. It said: 'Who knows? God may relent and change his mind; he may turn from his fierce anger, so that we do not perish' (Jonah 3).

Now can you really believe all that? Can you believe that God hadn't bargained for the reaction of these people? Can you believe that he had been set on ruining them and that he changed his mind because of their prayers? This is supposed to be God the Creator, who makes all things and keeps them in existence from moment to moment – not just like a sculptor, who makes a statue and leaves it alone, but like a singer who keeps her song in existence at all times. Can *he* really be manipulated by our prayers? You might think that he could if he were just a god from Olympus or Asgard. But we are now concerned with a Jewish story (the book of Jonah). And the Jews despised all such gods. They worshipped only the maker of heaven and earth, the maker of all things visible and invisible.

So some people think that the idea of praying to God to get what you want must be just primitive and superstitious and ought to stop. It is just childish to ask God for things. True, proper, grown-up Christian prayer should be just praise of God and thanksgiving. God knows what we need better than we do, and he will do the best for us as a loving Father. Didn't

Jesus say (cf. Matthew 6:8) that God knows what we need before we ask? So why bother asking?

Well for one thing, having told us that God knows what we need before we ask, Jesus gives us a specimen prayer (cf. Matthew 6:9–13). And it is full of asking for things: for bread, for forgiveness, for protection from evil. And Jesus also told us to pester God with our prayers, because God can be like a reluctant neighbour who has gone to bed and doesn't want to be bothered to get up and give us what we are shouting for (cf. Luke 11:5–8).

So what are we to think? We might, to start with, note that, when we pray, we should not be in too much of a hurry to think about God. We should think about ourselves and what we need. And we should present this before God. If you want to know why you should pray; the short answer is that God wants you to. And not because he craves for your attention and wants you to flatter him, but because he loves you and wants what is best for you and because praying is very good for you. Of course your prayer doesn't do anything for God, still less could it change God. God is just totally and absolutely and unconditionally in love with you and stays that way without a shadow of alteration. Prayer is good for us first of all because in prayer (I mean real prayer: asking for what we want) we understand more deeply that we are children of God and that he is our loving Father. And there is nothing selfish about that. It is normal human behaviour. What would you think of a child who never asked her parents for anything? What would her parents think of her? Would they think her to be unselfish? Or would they think her to be a dreadful little prig?

Of course you do have to pray for the right things. And some high-minded people say that this means not praying for vulgar material things like getting better from sickness, but only for spiritual goods like becoming more generous. In this they are very much mistaken and often, I think, a bit dishonest too. I suspect they prefer to pray for spiritual things because these are less visible and it's harder to check on whether their prayer has really been answered. No: when I say we must pray for the right things I don't mean that. I mean that we should pray for what we *want*, and not for what we just think we *ought* to want. Of course we commonly pray together and may all want different things. But notice how very careful the ancient liturgies are not to attribute to us longings and yearnings for high spiritual gifts or for any special desires except to have our sins forgiven and be on the way to heaven.

When you pray, consider what you want and need and never mind how vulgar or childish it might appear. If you want very much to pass that exam or get to know that girl or boy better, that is what you should pray for. You could let world peace rest for a while. You may not be ready yet to want that passionately. When you pray you must come before God as honestly as you can. There is no point in pretending to *him*. One of the great human values of prayer is that you face the facts about yourself and admit to what you want; and you know you can talk about this to God because he is totally loving and accepting. In true prayer you must meet God and meet yourself where you really are, for it is just by this that God will move you on from where you really are. For prayer is a bit of a risk. If you pray and acknowledge your most infantile desires, there is every danger that you may grow up a bit, that God will grow you up. When (as honestly as you can) you speak to God of your desires, very gently and tactfully he will often reveal to you that in fact you have deeper and more mature desires. But there is only one way to find this out: to start from where you are. It is no good pretending to yourself that you are full of high-minded aspirations. You have to wait until you are. If a child is treated as though she were already an adult, she will never become an adult. Prayer is the way in which our Father in heaven leads each of us by different paths to be saints, that is to say, with him.

There is no such thing as unanswered prayer (if it is real prayer, and not just going through the motions). Either God will give you what you ask, and this is extremely common; or else he will reckon that you are ready now to receive *more* than you asked. To you at the time, and especially to an outside observer, it may look as though your prayer has not been answered. But, as you will recognize some time later, God has been getting you to understand that your deeper desire was for more than you asked for. If you let this continue he will gradually lead you to realizing that what you really do want above all things is himself. Only God can reveal that to you, for only God can bring it about in you. I cannot tell you, and nor can anyone else. It is one of those things that 'flesh and blood' does not reveal to you but only your 'Father in heaven' (cf. Matthew 16:17). But the way to grow is to recognize that we have not yet grown. And God does not mind this at all. In fact, even if we do deceive ourselves, even if we are hypocrites, he will find ways of healing us.

People quite often say they are distracted during prayer. And they try to suppress these distractions. But this may well be a mistake. For distractions almost always come because we are praying for the wrong thing, because we are praying not for what we really want but for what we think we ought to want. The distractions are simply our real wants and desires intruding on the noble but bogus wants we are praying about. When you are visited by distractions, do not turn them away; turn yourself round and look at them; ask yourself what desires and worries and affections they come from. Then start praying about *that*. Once you are praying for what really concerns you, you will not be distracted. People on sinking ships complain of many things, but not of distractions during their prayers.

Well, what then about the problem we started with? Can we put pressure on God so that he changes his mind? No, of course we cannot. But the very question comes from thinking of prayer as something that starts from us, which it does not. Like everything else, it starts from God. It is God who decides that we shall pray. And it is God who answers our prayer giving us what we ask for or more than we ask, but never less than we ask.

'But surely' (you might say), 'if God decides that we shall pray then our prayer cannot be something that comes freely and spontaneously from us. We may think that we are acting freely when we pray, but, in reality, we must be just puppets of God.' It is natural to think along these lines. But that is because it is hard to think of God but easy to think of the gods. If God were one of the gods, a powerful, the most powerful, inhabitant of the universe, then if we did what *he* decided we should indeed not be doing what *we* decided. We should be his puppets, manipulated from outside by another being. But God is not an inhabitant of the universe. He is not another being alongside us and competing with us. God the Creator is author of the entire universe and of all that is in it. He is so far *outside* it that he is *in* every bit of it while not himself being a bit of it. He is not one of the beings. He is *within* every being keeping it in being. He is within you making you to be *you*. What you do freely you do from the depth within you that is yourself. But you also do it from the even greater depth within you that is God making you to be yourself. There are things in our universe that are not free but always moved by other things. And there are things like ourselves that are sometimes *not* determined by other creatures but are free. But God is the author of them all.

Everything we have is God's free gift to us. But just because *everything* is, we easily forget this truth. But God wants from time to time to remind us of it. He wants us to see his gifts for what they are. So he wants to give them to us as answers to our prayer. When God heals us miraculously in answer to prayer we get a privileged glimpse of the generosity of God. But God is no less generous in creating and sustaining the skill of doctors and nurses and the ingenuity of researchers into medical technology. Answers to prayer (and miracles) are not special acts of God's love. They are just the perpetual action of God's love made specially visible to us.

But in deciding that we shall pray, our Father in heaven is actually doing even more than this. He is not just giving his creatures a reminder of his love. For in prayer God is not just treating us as his creatures. He is treating us as his *children*, his children in Christ, who is eternally God the Child. When we pray we confront the Father *in* Christ, having the Spirit of Christ who is the love between Father and Son. In prayer we are living out the eternal dialogue of God as Parent and God as Child that we call God as Holy Spirit. That eternal dialogue entered our history in the prayer of Jesus: in his acceptance of death out of love for his Father and for us. For the cross was his prayer to the Father to effect what he had failed to do: to effect it through his loving acceptance of failure. And the Father's answer to that prayer was the resurrection, Christ's resurrection and ours. All our prayer is a sharing in the prayer of the cross. That is why the eucharist is the greatest of our prayers. For it is the sacrament of the cross, the sign of the cross.

Chapter 19

Rejoicing

Rejoice always, pray without ceasing, give thanks in all
circumstances; for this is the will of God in Christ Jesus for
you.

(1 Thessalonians 5:16)

One thing that may strike us as a little odd about this is that
we are actually *commanded* to rejoice; and that seems a strange
thing. Surely we are either rejoicing or we are not. It seems
peculiar to rejoice to order: 'On the word of command: start to
Rejoice!' But Paul calmly includes it within a whole list of
instructions: 'always seek to do good to one another and to all.
Rejoice always, pray without ceasing, give thanks in all
circumstances ...' (1 Thessalonians 5:15–16).

Well, it may not be as crazy as it sounds because when we
are rejoicing we are not just having a feeling. We are
expressing something in signs, in symbols. If you think about
it, it is no more odd to be told to *rejoice* than it is to be told to
pray. Of course, as everybody says, what matters in prayer is
not a lot of words but our *attitude* to God. Nevertheless, this
attitude has to be expressed in words and gestures. We express
our joy too in bodily signs, by dancing, singing, or laughing.
We shout for joy, or hug each other, or turn cartwheels. Just
how we express our happiness will of course depend on what
country we live in and the local customs and traditions. In
parts of Africa you would express it in highly sophisticated and

formalized dance. In parts of British suburbia, I believe they
manage it with a slight twitch of the upper lip.

Anyway, it is a matter of expression, of communication; a
kind of talking; but a much richer and more complex kind of
talking than just *telling* people that you are happy. It is a
telling that is also an *invitation* to share in the telling.

Rejoicing, celebrating, is something we most naturally do
with other people. We *can* rejoice just by ourselves, but it is
never altogether satisfactory. Like the woman in the parable
who has just found the money she lost (Luke 15:8–10), we
want to call on the neighbours and tell them all about it.

This is not some trivial sociological fact. It is very
important. For calling on the neighbours to celebrate together
is just the kind of calling together (*ecclesia*) that the Church is.
There are all sorts of ways of talking about the community that
is the Church. You can think of it as a people who share the
same beliefs, or all those who have been baptized, or even all
the people who more or less agree with the Pope. And so on.
But I think that, first of all, the Church is the people who invite
each other to rejoice together.

Rejoice always, *pray* constantly, give *thanks* in all circumstances. You might have expected Paul to put prayer first: 'the
Church is the people who pray together'; but he does not. It is
joy that comes first. And, whether or not this occurred to Paul,
it is profoundly important. Unless we are filled with joy we
cannot pray. And unless we pray we cannot give thanks.

There is the possibility here of a peculiarly horrible vision of
the Church: a vision that used to be popular, or anyway quite
fashionable, 30 years or so ago: the idea that true Christians
were people who smiled all the time – the kind of thing that
was satirized in the film *The Life of Brian* ('Always look on the
bright side . . .'). I say 'peculiarly horrible' because it proposed
that Christians went with fixed smiles through a world of war
and torture and starvation and disease. It proposed that
authentic Christians could not be shaken with grief, or
furiously angry, or desperately lonely and miserable. Yet the

gospels tell us that Jesus himself was all these things. When Lazarus died he wept uncontrollably (John 11:35). When he attacked the temple he was beside himself with rage (cf. John 2:13–17). In Gethsemane he was lonely and afraid (cf. Mark 14:32–42).

The trouble with that horrible vision is the shallowness and cheapness of the joy. You may remember that this is what Paul lambasted the Corinthians for (1 Corinthians 11:17–22). Rejoice always, pray constantly, give thanks. Prayer begins in rejoicing because we have found what we had lost; it culminates in thanksgiving, or, as we say in Greek, *eucharist*. But, in his first letter to the Corinthians, Paul complained that they were having their eucharist on the cheap. Their rejoicing was like the heartless feasting of the wealthy while, outside, the poor were hungry. 'When you come together, it is not really to eat the Lord's supper. For when the time comes to eat, each of you goes ahead with your own supper, and one goes hungry and another becomes drunk' (1 Corinthians 11:20–21). Paul says to them: Remember, it was precisely on the night when he was *betrayed* that the Lord Jesus took bread and gave thanks. The Corinthians are behaving like Judas and betraying Christ, siding with his executioners. Their joy is from the world. It is not the mysterious joy that comes from the cross itself. They are profaning the body and blood of the Lord.

So Christians are people who have a joy to express, but it is not the Corinthians' joy. It is a very special and profound joy, one that requires us to suffer with the suffering of the world. For this is the joy of *God*. It is the joy which *is* God. It is the joy which eternally bursts forth from God as he conceives of himself, speaking the word of his self-knowledge. In other words, it is the Spirit which proceeds from the Father through the Word. For us, it is the Joy, the Spirit, the New Life that is poured forth amongst humankind as that eternally spoken Word is made flesh and dwells amongst us.

And this is the sign that the Word of God was really made flesh, really dwelt amongst us in our world of fear and suspicion and envy: this is the sign that he gave himself to us utterly to do with him as we liked: *this* is the sign – *that we killed him*. The cross is our guarantee that God is not fooling in his love for us. He really did want to see himself, not only in his own eternal image, but in our image too, as one of us and, therefore, as part of our terrible world, part of the suffering, selfish, bickering world that we have made. And our joy is because God had such love for us; that he had such joy in being one with us; that he personally took on all the consequences of *being* one of us, of being love in a world of people not good at loving, people threatened by love.

So our joy, the joy that culminates in our thanksgiving, our eucharist, is joy in the cross. Our eucharist is 'the sign of the cross'. Sure, our joy is expressed in the ordinary symbols of human celebration: in a meal together, a party, a love-feast. But it is only an authentic love-feast if it expresses the love that wants to be *one* with, to *suffer* with, the suffering of all the world. It is an authentic love-feast only if it expresses our solidarity with the cross, our solidarity, not only with our companions and comrades, but with the victim who represents all the victims of the world. It is only if we die with Christ on the cross that we can share his life, his Spirit, which is the Joy of God.

And how do we share in the cross? Well the Corinthians show us how *not* to. Paul said they were betraying Christ because they forgot about the poor. We are also told about it most explicitly in the book of Isaiah:

> The spirit of the Lord God is upon me,
> because the Lord has anointed me;
> he has sent me to bring good news to
> the oppressed,
> to bind up the brokenhearted,
> to proclaim liberty to the captives,
> and release to the prisoners;
> to proclaim the year of the Lord's favour,

and the day of vengeance of our God;
to comfort all who mourn.

(Isaiah 61:1–2)

To find in the cross grounds for rejoicing is to have faith. It is to be able to say: 'This is where God is.' It is to rejoice in the cross – to rejoice in the torture and death of the man who was ready to be tortured and to die for the sake of being with all who suffer. And this is what the eucharist is: a rejoicing in the cross. The eucharist, and the rest of the sacramental life that surrounds it, are signs of faith, *sacramenta fidei* as the Church has traditionally called them. When we celebrate the eucharist we announce our faith that here, in what looks superficially like bread and wine, is indeed the body of Christ, who died to be with us out of love for us and out of loving obedience to his Father, who commanded him to love us. And beyond that we announce our faith that here in this suffering is where God is to be found. We say with the centurion in Mark: 'Truly this man was God's Son' (Mark 15:39).

We have this faith in the significance of the cross not because we have come to it and formed an opinion or reached a conclusion. We have it because the power which is in the weakness and defeat of the cross has come to us. The Spirit that, John says, Christ breathed forth in dying on the cross (John 19:30) has come to us in the form of joy, in the form of faith. This is where our Christian life begins. Inspired by this mysterious joy, which is the eternal Spirit of God, we can pray. We can call God 'Father' – not just 'Creator', but 'Father'. In this Spirit of joy we can act and speak as children of God, as Christ, the eternal Son, is Child of God.

So when we come in prayer and thanksgiving, when we come to make eucharist about the cross, we speak in the name of Christ, with the profound joy that Christ had even in the agony of his sacrifice. And God in hearing us is hearing the voice of his beloved son in whom he is well pleased.

Chapter 20

Trinity

Think for a moment of a group of three or four intelligent adults relaxing together in one of those conversations that have really taken off. They are being witty and responding quickly to each other – what in Ireland they call 'the Crack'. Serious ideas may be at issue, but nobody is being serious. Nobody is being pompous or solemn (nobody is preaching). There are flights of fancy. There are jokes and puns and irony and mimicry and disrespect and self-parody.

Now an intelligent 7-year-old is in the room, completely baffled by it all. She knows all these people have not gone mad. But she has no idea what is going on. The talk seems to have some kind of purpose. But it is not a purpose that she can grasp. Nobody is telling anybody anything. Nobody is doing anything. Above all nobody is doing anything about her. There are shouts of laughter, but there is no joke that she can understand. The room is full of joy and happiness, and she can see that. But she can't quite see why. Nobody is especially noticing her or telling her anything. And nobody is telling her off. It all seems baffling and utterly irrelevant.

Now this child is like us when we hear about the Trinity.

In fact what is going on with these adults is enormously relevant and important for the child; but not with a relevance and importance she can understand. It is important and relevant because no child is *just* a child; every child is growing up to be an adult, growing up to take part in the Crack. What is in fact most important to her is what she doesn't understand, though understands well enough that she wants to be grown-up. Her future destiny, her adult life is waiting for her, but she will only understand it when she takes part in it.

No child is *just* a child; no human being is *just* a human being. The child is on the way to sharing in a mysterious grown-up life. All human beings are on the way to sharing in a mysterious divine life. The child is on the way to sharing the life of her parents who made her. We are all on the way to sharing the life of God who made us.

But, for the child, grown-up life is not completely dark and unintelligible. The future life that she cannot understand, but is waiting for, is foreshadowed in the present life she *can* understand. The life of grown-ups among themselves is foreshadowed in the care that adults take of her. The friendship and joy and love amongst grown-ups is at least represented by the loving attention and care that is shown to her. That is something she can understand.

Just as the child gets glimpses of what adult life can be from the interest that grown-ups take in her, so all human beings can get glimpses of what divine life can be from the interest that God takes in us. That interest, that care and attention, is the whole story that is told in the Bible, from the creation of humankind to the sending of God's son to be one of us, to die for us, to be raised from the dead, and to send his Spirit of love and joy amongst us.

What do we learn from this story about what God had done for us? First that God so loved us that he sent his Son to us. That, for us, is a glimpse, a picture, of God the eternal *Parent*. Second, the Son, having become human, one of us for our sake, is obedient to his Father and the mission his Father has given him. That, for us, is a glimpse, a picture of God the eternal *Child*. Third, in response to this obedience, an obedience even unto the death of the cross, God, having raised Jesus from the dead, and brought him, this human being, to share in his divine joy, allows this divine joy to spill out from Jesus upon all his sisters and brothers: the first disciples are filled with the joy of the Spirit. That, for us, is a glimpse, a picture, of God the eternal *Joy*.

In eternity God brings forth his understanding of himself, his conception of himself, his image of himself, as the child is conception and image of the parent. And this is represented in our history by the coming of Jesus, Son of God (a coming in poverty, weakness and peril because that is the sort of world we have made). All that we celebrate at Christmas.

In eternity, God the Child, who is the very image of his Father, is eternally dependent on his life-giving parent for his whole being. He comes forth from the Father. And this is represented in our history by the loving obedience of the Word made flesh (an obedience unto suffering, torture and death because that is the sort of world we have made). All that we celebrate in Holy Week and Easter.

In eternity, God the Parent breathes forth the Joy he takes in his image, his Child, the reproduction of his divine life: and this is represented in our history by the breathing forth of the Spirit (a Spirit of joy, but also of struggle against the powers of evil, a struggle for justice and peace, because that is the sort of world we have made). All that we celebrate at Pentecost.

So, God sent us his Son: that is our way of entering the mystery of God the eternal Parent. The Son, Jesus, is obedient to his Father: that is our way of entering the mystery of God the eternal Child. Because of the obedience of his incarnate Word, his beloved Son, God is well pleased: that is our way of entering into the mystery of God the eternal Joy. God the eternal Parent; God the eternal Child; God the eternal Joy: God the Father; God the Son; God the Holy Spirit. This is the life of God. This is the life we look forward to sharing, as the child looks forward to sharing in grown-up life, sharing in the Crack. It does not matter that we do not understand it; it does not matter that we only get hints and glimpses of it in the story of Jesus; it does not matter that we cannot imagine how we could attain it. For God the Father, through his Son, is even now sending us the Holy Spirit so that we shall ourselves live that life of love and joy for eternity.

Chapter 21

The Forgiveness of God

What does forgiveness mean? It is one of those familiar, obvious things that we don't usually stop to examine. But if we are going to extend the word to try to talk about God (as Christians do), then it helps to be as clear about its ordinary use as we can be.

You forgive someone for an offence. But what exactly is an offence? I think that you are offended by someone who treats you like dirt – I mean someone who treats you as unimportant, not to be reckoned with, not someone in your own right. If Fred knocks you off your bike, and immediately stops and enquires solicitously for you, and helps you pick up the bike, and so on, you are hurt all right, but not offended. Think how different it would be if Fred just drives on laughing. The physical hurt may be exactly the same, but the offence would be enormously greater. Someone can compensate you for an *injury*, as between friends. But an *insult* goes much deeper. For that you need an apology, while an insult requires forgiveness.

It is when an injury becomes an insult that it is really an offence and needs forgiveness. And the reason for this, I think, is that an insult threatens us at a very deep level. It plays on our deep, nagging anxiety and fear that we don't matter, that we mean nothing. People who insult you don't care what you think, don't respect you as having your own life, don't take you seriously as a separate centre of feeling and thinking and living. They treat you as a *thing* that they can deal with. And their doing so threatens us because it awakens echoes in our own insecurity. Very deep in us is the fear that our existence as a subject is precarious, and contingent, and perhaps an illusion. The fact that we matter is not an obvious thing we can take for granted – like the fact that we have two hands. I don't mean that we doubt it all the time, though I suppose neurotic people do. I mean that the sense that we are *somebody* is vulnerable. And an insult attacks it directly.

So when people insult us, they become enemies. They do not just become people whose interests conflict with ours. That problem can be adjusted. The problem with people who insult us is that they become enemies of our existence. They treat us as a thing. And our first reaction is to deal with them and to force them to recognize that we do matter. That is what vengeance is: forcing your enemy to take you seriously, making it clear that you are not to be ignored. And, of course, this means treating your enemy as a thing, as someone to be dealt with.

An apology is meant to undo an insult. When Fred, who knocked you off your bike, stops and comes back to you, he apologizes of course. But that is not a real apology. Fred is simply trying to show that the injury he did was not an insult, that no apology is really needed. He does not abase himself or grovel before you. He simply means: 'No offence meant, no need to feel threatened or angry, let's get down to sensible, practical, superficial things like compensation and so on.' But a real apology comes when offence *has* been meant, when you have been insulted and demeaned and made to feel like dirt. And people who apologize really do abase themselves. They subject themselves. They say 'I know I have treated you like dirt. But here I am. Treat me like dirt if you like. I recognize your right to take vengeance. But I ask you not to.' To apologize is to ask for *grace* and to acknowledge that you have in no way deserved any consideration. Lots of animals have techniques or signals for turning away wrath, for exhibiting aggression, and so on. But only sign-using, linguistic animals

120

can really apologize. For only such animals can really insult. Only such animals have this deep anxiety about their own significance that an insult plays on.

When someone apologizes we sometimes say: 'Don't give it a thought; I wasn't offended.' And to speak like this is to claim to be so secure as not to be insulted in the first place. But real forgiveness comes when you have been insulted. Real forgiveness is a creative act of love. When offenders abase themselves, forgiveness is an act of grace which gives back to them their self-respect. It reassures them that they are loved. It enables them to be themselves again.

That happens when someone apologizes to you and the apology is really lovingly accepted. This is real creative reconciliation and, of course, it has to take place in visible signs, in rituals of apology and symbols of forgiveness. When this happens, the one who insulted you is recreated. He or she dies and is born again. And the relations between the two of you may well end up better than they were in the first place.

It is of course possible for you to forgive people when they do not apologize and are not sorry. You can forgive the enemies who remain your enemies. And this is real forgiveness. But of course it does not affect them. It does not redeem and recreate them. It is only if they go through a death and resurrection in the signs of apology and acceptance that they are affected.

Now all these platitudes may help us understand the forgiveness of God. God, of course, is not injured or insulted or threatened by our sin. So, when we speak of him forgiving, we are using the word 'forgiving' in a rather stretched way, a rather far-fetched way. We speak of God forgiving not because he is really offended but accepts our apology or agrees to overlook the insult. What God is doing is like forgiveness not because of anything that happens in God, but because of what happens in us, because of the *re-creative* and *redemptive* side of forgiveness. All the insult and injury we do in sinning is to ourselves alone, not to God. We speak of God forgiving us because he comes to us to save us from ourselves, to restore us after we have injured ourselves, to redeem and re-create us.

We can forgive enemies even though they do not apologize and are not contrite. But such forgiveness, as I have said, does not help them, does not re-create them. In such forgiveness *we* are changed, we change from being vengeful to being forgiving, but our enemy does not change. When it comes to God, how-ever, it would make no sense to say he forgives the sinner without the sinner being contrite. For God's forgiveness just *means* the change he brings about in the sinner, the sorrow and repentance he gives to the sinner. God's forgiveness does not mean that God changes from being vengeful to being forgiving, God's forgiveness does not mean any change what-ever in God. It just means the change in the sinner that God's unwavering and eternal love brings about.

The expression of our forgiveness may just be something we say to ourselves which our enemies do not know about or care about and which does nothing for them. Such forgiveness is good for us; it blesses him that gives, even though not him that takes. The expression of God's forgiveness could never be just something God says to himself; it can only be the repentance of the sinner, the death and resurrection of the sinner. For God to forgive us *is* for us to repent. We just have different names for the same thing. But there is no real gap between the two. Someone might apologize sincerely to you, and you might refuse to accept his or her apology. Indeed, if that were not possible, there could be no true apology (if resurrection is not an unmerited grace there could be no true death). But it would make no sense to speak of God as refusing to accept our repentance. Our repentance *is* God's forgiveness of us.

The coming into us of God's own life of love shows itself in two aspects: our repentance, and our being forgiven, our death to our sins, and our new life of love. It is not at all that God waits for us to be repentant before he will condescend to forgive us, like someone saying: 'I'll forgive him provided he apologizes.' We do not express our contrition in order to *persuade* God to grant us his forgiveness. Our contrition *is* God granting us forgiveness. Of course, the form of words or signs that we (or, at least, most of my Christian friends) use can give the impression that God needs persuading, that we must beg him for forgiveness, that we should plead for him to turn his anger from us, and so on. But all that is just metaphor, a figure of speech. We speak to God *as though* he were someone we had insulted or offended, and we have no other suitable way of praying; there is nothing wrong with performing *Hamlet* so long as you don't call in the police half way through and have Claudius arrested for murder. *Not* to express our contrition in some such way would simply be a sign that our contrition is bogus, and therefore that it is not really the forgiveness of God.

Our sins being forgiven is not, then, distinct from the other manifestations of the life of God in us, the life of love which expresses itself in our forgiving others. It is not that God refuses to forgive our sins unless we first forgive those that have sinned against us. That is only a picturesque way of talking. Our forgiving others is the work of God's forgiveness in us. It is not that God refuses to forgive us unless we forgive others. It would be logically impossible for him to do so. God's act of forgiveness is not a change in him. It is simply the change by which we become, for example, forgiving instead of vengeful. If we remain vengeful, then that is because we have not accepted the forgiveness of God, that we are not yet forgiven.

All that God asks of us is that we put aside the barriers, the illusions and the timidity that stand in the way of accepting his love. All that he asks is that we relax and let ourselves be filled with his love, which eliminates our sins and makes us channels and bearers of his love and forgiveness to everyone.

Chapter 22

Render to Caesar

Broadly speaking, Christians can be divided into two kinds: those who have to try to explain away all those things Jesus says about rich people not being able to enter the kingdom, and how the kingdom belongs only to the poor, and those who have to try to explain away the gospel story about paying tribute to Caesar (Matthew 22:15–22; Mark 12:13–17; Luke 20:20–26). This story, in all its versions, seems to say that the service of God has nothing to do with rich and poor, nothing to do with class-struggle, nothing to do with politics and all that. It seems to say that all of that belongs to the emperor, to Caesar. Jesus appears to be envisaging two kinds of service in which we are involved: public life (the things that belong to Caesar, especially things connected with money), and another kind of life (private life perhaps) – the things that have to do with God. He seems to be saying that when it comes to voting, or any other kind of political or economic activity, we can leave God out of it. He also seems to be saying that when it comes to the service of God we can forget about politics and economics.

Many Christians are quite happy about this. For them, the worship of God is essentially a private affair, or, anyway, the concern only of small informal groups who don't interfere with anyone else, who don't want to be interfered with, who just want to be let alone to worship God in their own way. And there are many politicians who would like to be left alone to get on with the pragmatic business of government. These

125

people don't want to interfere with religion. They don't want bishops and the like to interfere with them. Such people, I think, are especially affected by periods when the mixing of God and politics has produced disastrous explosions, when the Church has just been persecuted, when clerics have had their grip on the political process, or when sectarian feelings have been exploited for political purposes. People who have been hurt often just want to be left alone.

And you can understand such politicians' point of view. Mixing God with things can be extremely dangerous. God is an unpredictable explosive substance, and when he is around people are likely to get hurt, even crucified. The best thing to do with God is to insulate him carefully inside churches, or, better still, inside small groups of like-minded devout people. And Jesus in the 'Render to Caesar' story really does seem to lend some support to this view. Give to Caesar the things that are Caesar's (on weekdays) and to God the things that are God's (on Sundays).

Yet what of the following?

In our country one million families live in houses held to be unfit for human habitation. More than double that number are living in sub-standard houses. There is evidence that in the last two or three years the prices of moderate-sized houses in some areas has doubled. The compulsory increase in the rents of council houses is inevitably reflected in the increased rents of privately owned rented accommodations.[1]

Whose language is this? It obviously has to do with things that are Caesar's. But it comes from a statement issued by British bishops.

---

[1] *Homelessness: A Fact and a Scandal* (report published in 1990 by the Department for Christian Social Responsibility and Citizenship of the [Roman Catholic] Bishops' Conference of England and Wales).

Have the bishops got the whole thing wrong? Are they dabbling in politics when they should be looking after the souls of their flocks? They certainly seem to be dabbling in politics. They go on to 'urge Christian societies and parish organizations to ... make representations locally to secure some easement or control for the house prices and rents'. If that means anything, it means that some Christians are being urged by their bishops to take part in campaigns against local council authorities.

Well now imagine someone coming to see Jesus asking him: 'Look, should we pay this increased rent or not?' And imagine him replying: 'Show me the rent-book. Whose name is here as landlord? The Council's? Well render to the Council the things that are the Council's, and to God the things that are God's.' Does that mean, 'Yes, pay what you are told to pay, and then go away and pray'?

Maybe, but that isn't what the bishops say. They don't say a word about praying. They first of all try to make sure their own house is in order. They tell diocesan authorities and religious orders to hand over any spare land or buildings they have to housing associations and local authorities (not, of course, to private enterprise) to make homes. And then they talk about putting pressure on local councils and finding ways to reduce what they call 'the hardships and injustices arising from this grave social evil'.

Now most of us, I suppose, want to raise a small cheer when we hear bishops saying things like that. They don't often do this, though they do it a lot more often than they are given credit for, and a lot more often than they used to. But the point is that if we cheer the bishops, what are we to say about Jesus? Doesn't he teach that bishops as such, people concerned with the service of God, should keep themselves quite separate from the affairs of Caesar? So let's look at our gospel story more carefully, just in case this isn't what Jesus is saying.

The first thing we need to do is to question our easy assumption that Caesar stands as a symbol for the political sphere, for the civil power, for the secular world of power and money. Caesar was an actual historical person, and the scene depicted in our story takes place in a definite historical context. If we forget about the context, it won't be surprising if we misinterpret the scene. If we have the idea that Jesus wandered about the peaceful hills of Galilee, or the bustling town of Jerusalem, where people went about their business in an ordinary way under the benign, but strict, rule of Rome and the Herodian family, we have the thing more than slightly wrong.

Jesus lived and preached and died in the run-up to an extremely bloody and unsuccessful colonial uprising. The actual revolutionary war did not take place for another 30 years or so, but already in the time of Jesus there were underground revolutionary movements, illegal armies, acts of terrorism and hideous acts of repression. The country was held down by a large Roman army who, like all armies of occupation, bullied and harassed the people. The Romans maintained as their local puppet-ruler (besides their own governor) the family of Herod, who did not come from the culture and background of the natives, and whose power depended on maintaining the union with Rome.

So the Herodians mentioned in this story (they are there in Matthew and Mark's version anyway) were collaborationists with the colonial regime. The Pharisees on the other hand (also mentioned only by Matthew and Mark) were deeply devoted to the national Jewish tradition, to its law and culture. They were profoundly conscious that the Jewish people were called to be the people of God. They believed that the Roman occupation was a blasphemy, and that their fellows belonged not to Caesar but only to God. The Pharisees, you might say, identified the Kingdom of God with the Jewish people (once it had been liberated and come to its full power). This, indeed, is how the Kingdom of God is pictured by some of the Old Testament prophets: Jerusalem ruling the world and spreading its peace and justice to all the nations who flock to her to serve Yahweh.

The Pharisees and Herodians, then, were bitter enemies. They were not merely people who disagreed in an academic sort of way. They were fierce political opponents (at least, the Pharisees were fierce; the Herodians tended to be rather easygoing, as people are when their security and privilege is guaranteed by a large army). The Pharisees tended to be more fanatical and narrow-minded, as subversive groups often are. And it is this fanaticism that we hear most about in the gospels. But it is not the whole story. On approximately the same side as the Pharisees were the Zealots: various groups of militant revolutionary activists who carried out ambushes and generally harassed the occupying forces. Their ideology doesn't seem to have been very different from that of the Pharisees. They were fanatical, pious nationalists. The Zealots were an illegal underground movement and, of course, they would not have dreamt of paying taxes to Rome. I expect they intimidated people who did pay taxes, or levied taxes themselves in the villages, as most guerrilla forces do. The Pharisees were, of course respectable and respected people. However much they might secretly approve of the Zealots' attitude to taxes, they could hardly say so openly. They would have been imprisoned or crucified for doing so.

It is now clear why Jesus calls them hypocrites and says, 'Why are you putting me to the test?' (Matthew 22:18; cf. Mark 12:15). The Pharisees have recognized, of course, that the teaching of Jesus is subversive. But it is not only subversive of the political order. It is much more directly subversive of the religious order. The Pharisees see Jesus as putting forward alien and blasphemous ideas that would destroy the national tradition. They view him as a threat to themselves and to everything that makes their lives meaningful. So they propose to betray him to the common enemy: the Roman forces of occupation. That's why Jesus calls them hypocrites. They tacitly, or in private, give support to the Zealot cause. But they are hypocritically asking Jesus to come out and declare support for it in public. And, to make things quite sure, they arrange for some Herodians to be around while he does it. 'We know you are not afraid of anyone, you believe in simply speaking your mind. Come on, stand up and be counted.'

Jesus is in a difficult position. He will either announce his support for the Zealots (and the Herodians will gleefully take this news back to the Roman police), or else he will have to throw in his lot with the upper-class Herodians, admit that what he had to say is irrelevant to the struggle going on, and lose the young people – people like Simon the Zealot and others who form part of his following – and in fact lose his popular support altogether.

Jesus, of course, is quite prepared to lose his popular support, but not on these terms, not as a collaborationist Herodian. When he does come to die, deserted by practically everyone except his mother, it is at the hands of the Romans and Herodians, betrayed by the nationalists.

This is the difficulty Jesus is in, and we misunderstand his extremely clever reply if we think he simply opts for the Herodian position. If we think that Jesus is simply saying 'my gospel is separate from politics', then he is simply taking the Herodian side. But this is not what he says at all. This wouldn't account for the conclusion of our gospel story: 'They were amazed' (Matthew 22:22); 'They were utterly amazed at him' (Mark 12:17); 'Being amazed by his answer, they became silent' (Luke 20:26). It would not have been particularly surprising if Jesus had taken the side of the collaborationists. It would merely have been a little dull. What he, in fact, does is extricate himself with a witty phrase. And the point of the phrase is that it could be understood either way.

It could be a revolutionary Zealot slogan: 'Let Caesar take what is his, but this people belongs to God. Let Caesar have his petty little empire in the rest of the world, but this land and this people is to be ruled by no one but God himself and his law, given directly to us.' This reading, of course, is emphasized by the coin of the tribute that has a representation of Caesar on it (the kind of graven image that was strictly forbidden by Jewish law). The Jews were forbidden to make images of the human form. The coins of God's tribute are the living coins stamped with God's image. The only image of God for the Jews is man. Let Caesar lay claim to his human possessions, but not to this people. Let God claim what is his and smash the power of these blasphemers who dare to tread on the Holy Ground of Israel. In other words: 'Romans Go Home, where you belong.'

On the other hand, Jesus's phrase could be read as an Herodian slogan (in the way that we have so often been taught to read it): 'Pay your taxes and keep religion out of public life; keep it as a private personal indulgence.'

But, of course, Jesus is not just extricating himself neatly from a trap. After all, in the final showdown he doesn't bother to extricate himself at all. He allows himself to be betrayed by the nationalists to the colonial power. He is not just wriggling out of a difficult situation with a kind of 'No Comment'. He wants to say that the question he is put is the wrong one. The quarrel between Herodians and Pharisees, between collabora-tionists and the resistance, is not the ultimate struggle. The liberation he has come to bring goes beyond political liberation. Jesus stood out against the Zealots and the Pharisees not because he was a Herodian, and not just because he rightly judged that when it came to the final confrontation they would lose and Jerusalem would be worse off than ever, but because they were fighting the wrong fight, fighting in the name of a distortion of the Jewish tradition and, therefore, a distortion of the Word of God.

They were fighting against the forces and idols of paganism in the name of a God they had appropriated to the national tradition, the God of the Law. Jesus has come to show them that this too is an idol, that the real liberation of people lies in the faith that God is he who loves us, he who ultimately and unconditionally loves us (not because we are Jewish, or Christian or revolutionaries, but because we are who we are).

This is the terrifying and destructive love of God which

makes us able to see who we are, which smashes our own idols, our images of ourselves, and makes us confess our sin. And, in doing so, it liberates us, raises us from the dead to a new and free life in the Spirit of love. The Kingdom of which Jesus speaks is not to be achieved just by defeating Roman domination (or by replacing it by the Jewish Law, or by the authority of the Church). The Kingdom is fully achieved only when Jesus will hand over the Kingdom to God the Father, having done away with every sovereignty, authority and power, so that God may be all in all.

Chapter 23

Mammon and Thanksgiving

> No one can serve two masters; for a slave will either hate the
> one and love the other, or he will be devoted to the one and
> despise the other. You cannot serve God and wealth.
>
> (Matthew 6:24)

You cannot both serve God and serve money, says Jesus. Well
first an elementary logical point: it does follow from this that if
you are serving God, you cannot be serving money. Nor does it
follow from this that if you are not serving God, you must be
serving money. You may be doing neither. We all know people
whose lives are spent in the service of scholarship, or who are
dedicated to political liberation, or who are simply head-over-
heels in love, who are not serving either God or money. The
fact that they are not out for personal profit does not, I'm
afraid, mean that they are, in some hidden way, unbeknownst
to themselves, serving God. They may be admirable people in
various respects, but they are not necessarily serving God. But,
of course, they *may* be. What Jesus is saying is that if you are
serving money (unlike scholarship, or the revolution, or your
girlfriend), if you are serving money, then you *cannot* be serving
God. Whatever we mean by God and the service of God, it is
something incompatible with serving money, though it is not
incompatible with serving other things (at least, Jesus doesn't
say it is).

So, perhaps if we look into what serving money means we

may come to understand something about what serving God means. First, let us be clear that for Matthew, and for Jesus, the word we translate as 'wealth' or 'money' (*mammon*) didn't mean what it means for us. Because of this passage in Matthew, and the similar one in Luke (Luke 16:13), we have come to use the word to mean a kind of false god of money, standing for greed and rapacity. But for the writers of the gospels it simply meant money – not something that obviously bad.

So what is Jesus saying here? Some people say that Jesus is making a contrast between being concerned with material things (money) and being concerned with non-material things (spiritual things). But this isn't what he says.

He doesn't contrast material and spiritual things. The contrast he goes on to make is between two material things: the body and its clothing: 'Is not ... the body more than clothing?' (Matthew 6:25) And, in any case, being concerned about spiritual things (scholarship let's say) is not at all the same as being concerned about God.

In this part of Matthew's gospel Jesus doesn't talk about spiritual things at all – unless you reckon money itself as a spiritual thing. And, if you think about it, money is a good deal more spiritual than bread or beer or your body. Money isn't, in any important way, a thing at all. It is a power over things, and a power over people. After the experience of inflation it is easy to see that what matters about money is not how much there is of it but how much power it has (the same is true of beer, but that's in a different sense).

So Jesus isn't contrasting having to do with material things and having to do with something else. He is contrasting two ways of having to do with things (whether they are material or not): the way represented by serving money, and the way represented by serving God. The way of power, and the way of thanksgiving. The way of acquisition, and the way of the eucharist.

'Is not life more than food, and the body more than clothing?'

(Matthew 6:25) The contrast here is not between spiritual and material. Neither is it between something important and something trivial. It is a contrast between what you are and what you then have. You *are* a body; you *have* a hat. Of course we speak of 'having' a body too, but obviously you don't have a body the way you have a hat. You don't wear your body on anything; it is what you wear things on.

So there is a difference between the material thing that you are, your living body, and the material things you have, like hats and sandwiches and houses. And the second ones are important only because of the first.

Jesus is saying: 'Look, you didn't get the first important thing, the thing that makes everything else important, by worrying about and striving for it: Your bodily existence is free gift from your heavenly Father. If he provides that as free gift to you, do you not think that he provides all the rest as well?'

Of course, to take that question on board depends on remembering that what and who you are is gift from your heavenly Father. If we forget that we are gift from God, if we forget, so to say, what comes before us, what is presupposed to us being here at all, if we simply take our lives, ourselves, as our base-line, so to speak, as where we start from, then life is about what we have and what we can get.

Of course, we need food and clothes. And of course we have to get them to live. But Jesus is asking us to remember the much more fundamental sense in which we have to have God to live. But for the first gift of God, our lives and bodies, we should not even need food. It is not just the gift of God that we have food; it is even the gift of God that we are hungry – that we are there at all to stand in need of anything.

Jesus is not recommending that we just sit around waiting for God to put food in our mouths instead of getting it ourselves. Certainly the birds of the air don't do that (cf. Matthew 6:26). And I don't think the lilies of the field do either (cf. Matthew 6:28). Jesus is reminding us that our very selves, including our work and our struggles, are God's gift.

In one sense we depend on food and clothes. And the proper response to this is to acquire some. In another, and deeper, sense we depend on God. And the proper response to this is to thank him. And this is to *serve* him. Serving God isn't doing anything for him, as though he needed our help. It is recognizing his gift to us, recognizing ourselves as his gift, thanking him.

When, forgetting this, we see our lives simply as what *we* have done, what we have acquired and achieved (or failed to acquire and achieve), how we have, or have not, power over things and people, then we are giving to money (the power over things) the service of thanksgiving that is due to God.

The attitude that goes with giving to God the service of thanksgiving that belongs to him is joy and peace. We can thank God for our food when we have it. But we can even thank him when we haven't it. We can thank him for being alive enough to be hungry. But if we give this service to money, our attitude oscillates between self-congratulation when we have succeeded and anxious worry that we should fail. For to fail would now be to lose the meaning of our lives; for now life's meaning would lie in what power we can exercise.

If we serve God, we are recognizing that what matters first is what we receive and not what we do or make. What matters first is that we are loved. And this we have before anything we deserve or achieve. To understand this is to understand that it is not only our deeds and our works that matter, but that we matter ourselves. We matter, not first because of what we have made of ourselves, but because of what God has made of us. And that includes what we make of ourselves. To serve God is to stop congratulating ourselves and to begin to love ourselves: to love ourselves as God loves us: not for being rich or clever or powerful, but just for being ourselves. And when we know God's love for us, and when we can love ourselves, then we can share in God's love for others. Unless we serve God, unless we thank him for our being, unless we love ourselves, whatever we do for others will not be love. It may be admirable enough in its own way. It may simply be a delight in doing what we are good at. Or it may be a more sinister delight in the exercise of power over others. But, whether it is good, or whether it is sinister, it will not be love: not that love which is a sharing in God's love for us.

Serving God does not mean that we do not try to succeed, to exercise power, to achieve what is good and necessary. It means that, whether we succeed or fail, we search into our life to detect in it the love from God which is sustaining us both in success and failure. Sometimes this task is clear and easy, and sometimes it is obscure and dark. Sometimes we can see nothing of the love of God; sometimes even life itself does not look like God's gift. And then we simply know it is so, even though we do not see even a glimpse of it. We know this because the eternally beloved Son of God himself was poor and a failure; because he emptied himself, was a slave, and died the death of a slave. And it was just in the darkness of this failure that the Father's love for him appeared to us and is shared with us.

Chapter 24

Transfiguration

> Jesus took with him Peter and James and his brother John and led them up a high mountain, by themselves. And he was transfigured before them, and his face shone like the sun, and his clothes became dazzling white.
>
> (Matthew 17:1–2; cf. Mark 9:2–3 and Luke 9:28–9)

As usual, it's quite important to see where the account of Jesus's Transfiguration comes in Matthew's gospel. In Matthew, and for that matter in Mark and Luke as well, the story of the Transfiguration comes immediately after Peter's crucial proclamation of faith: that Jesus is the Messiah, the Son of the living God. Notice first of all that this comes pretty late in all three gospels. It is quite a long time before Jesus is prepared to let people say that he is Messiah. We are inclined to be a bit superior about this and say, 'Well, you see the Jews, the disciples, had rather simple-minded notions about the Messiah; they thought he would be a political figure who would restore the fortunes of Israel. So Jesus had to make it clear first of all that he was a spiritual leader, that being Messiah meant something quite different. He had to make this clear before he could allow anyone to say that he was Messiah.' I say we are inclined to say this in a superior sort of way, as if the poor Jews were all wrong though we can see the matter much more clearly. We don't have any of these illusions about the Messiah being a political figure, so it is easy for us to understand what Jesus meant by being the Messiah, the Christ.

But, if we do say this kind of thing, it is we who are wrong. The reason why Jesus delayed so long before admitting to being the Messiah was not just because the Jews were making a mistake. He didn't have to wait simply in order to clear up their ideas. The real reason why he delayed and waited was to give people time to get to know him. And this matters for us, just as much as it mattered for the Jews. The fact is that people cannot begin to understand what it means to say 'Jesus is the Christ' or 'Jesus is Lord' or 'Jesus is Son of the Living God' until they have spent some time getting to know *Jesus* himself. It is not just a question of getting rid of one mistaken idea of what being Messiah means. It is not as though we had to get rid of a mistaken concept and replace it by the correct one. The thing is that getting to know Jesus means putting *all* our concepts under judgement – I mean all our concepts of what is meant by 'Christ' or 'Lord' or 'Son of God'. In meeting Jesus we see that none of them will really do.

We can try to explain what life is all about, what the point of existence or human history is. We can try to explain this using words like 'God' (borrowed from old religions), or we can use expressions like 'the Messiah', 'the Christ', 'the anointed One', 'the Spirit-bearer' (borrowed from the Old Testament tradition). But when we encounter Jesus of Nazareth we realize that none of these words or expressions are good enough. None of them really say what we want to assert about him or ourselves, or what we want to say to him. To succeed in any way here we have to get to know Jesus. And this can be quite a long process (it took quite a long time for the disciples). Even when Peter says that Jesus is the Christ, and Jesus lets him get away with it, Peter immediately shows that he hasn't really grasped what it is all about. He hasn't really seen that being Messiah is not a matter or achieving something, but of failure. Jesus tries to explain that he must suffer and die, but Peter cries out 'God forbid it, Lord! This must never happen to you' (Matthew 16:22). And Jesus turns on him saying 'Get behind me, Satan! . . . You are setting your mind not on divine things but on human things' (Matthew 16:23).

In fairness to Peter, he is appalled because he at least understands what Jesus is saying in a way that we often do not. When Jesus says he must suffer many things and be killed (Matthew 16:21) we are inclined to think: 'Oh yes, the significance of Jesus is to be shown forth not by any easy success but by the heroic way in which he faces suffering and death; the victory will be one of heroism in the face of overwhelming force.' We think of the victory of the cross in terms of toughness and endurance. But Jesus is not doing so. Heroism is only another kind of human achievement. And the point of the cross is not that it is any kind of achievement. It is not heroic; it is absurd. Jesus is saying (and Peter understands this) not that he is going to have a heroic courageous death but that he is going to be defeated, going to fail, to be humiliated. This is what shocks Peter and this is what would shock us if we really grasped it.

We try to avoid thinking this. We are always trying to find ways in which Jesus wins. If we can't see him as politically successful, then we think of him as spiritually successful. If he wasn't a conquering hero, then he was a heroic martyr who triumphed over his persecutors by his calm resignation in the face of suffering. But he didn't, of course. He broke down and wept and sweated with terror in the garden of Gethsemane. He wasn't a spiritual success either. By the end he had no disciples left. They had all deserted him. Jesus was an outstanding failure. And that is how he shows us the meaning of God. That is what the Transfiguration is about.

Just before he gets to his account of the Transfiguration, Matthew has Jesus saying: 'If any want to become my followers, let them deny themselves' (Matthew 16:24). That is not calling on us to exercise the human virtue and excellence of self-control and restraint. It is asking us to deny ourselves, to deny the *ultimate* value of all human excellence and virtue. If we want to save our lives, we must lose them.

It is only when we see the Transfiguration in this context that we understand it. For, of course, Jesus is not being nihilistic. He is not being ultimately pessimistic. He is not saying that nothing is worth anything, that ultimate truth is nothingness and destruction and failure. Or, at least, if he is saying this, he is also giving us hope beyond anything we can see as ultimate. He reveals the love that is deeper than the most ultimate human love, the love that is God. If we are prepared to accept our own uselessness, if we can face the fact that we are going to fail, if we can glimpse what death means and recognize that we are going to die, if we are prepared to be as worthless, as useless, as Jesus Christ, then we will encounter God; then we will be in touch with life beyond anything we can mean by 'life'. For the meaning of God is found in suffering, in baptism.

The Transfiguration is a repetition of the scene at the baptism of Jesus, with the same voice coming from heaven: and this is because the suffering of Jesus is to be seen as a baptism, a new life as well as a destruction of the old. The Transfiguration has all the apparatus of a manifestation of God such as you get in the Old Testament. We have the shining light, the usual injunction 'Fear not', and, of course, Moses and Elijah are there to indicate that this suffering, this baptism of Jesus, is in fulfilment of the Law and the prophets. The point being made is that it really is God (the God who was the key to everything for the Old Testament) who is to be found in the kind of failure that the cross is.

And this is not the kind of spectacular failure that we all really know is a success. It is just the common or garden failure that comes of being human. Jesus died of being human. What was outstanding about him was not that he was something more than human, that he was superman or superstar. It was just that he was more intensely human, more intensely one of us than we dare to be. He lacked the illusions and deceptions by which we try to protect ourselves from our humanity, try to protect ourselves from our failure. He was like to us in all things but sin, in all things but self-deception. He shows us God simply by showing us the reality of being human. And it is not at all the reality we like to think it is. Really being human is not at all like what humanists believe in their simple-minded way. Really being human means being in the kind of muddle and mess that Jesus was in. And this is where God is.

It was absolutely characteristic of Peter that he should try once again to grasp the divinity without the failure. The flash of divinity, the glimpse of meaning, only comes out of the failure, out of the cross. But we find Peter wanting to *fix* the moment of revelation. His suggestion is: Let's build three tents and preserve this moment (cf. Matthew 17:4). How often Peter and his successors have gone in for building, trying to preserve the lightening flash of divinity in solid and permanent form, almost forgetting that this flash only comes from the darkness of failure and death. Almost forgetting, for again it is characteristic of Peter that he somehow recovers, he is tempted, and falls, and is picked up again. When they lifted up their eyes they saw only Jesus (Matthew 17:8). In the end Peter knows, and the Church knows, that *there is only Jesus*, that the meaning of God is to be found only in the one man who was man. There is no place to find God except in man, and no way to find man except in Jesus Christ. Idolaters and pagans, and religious people generally, think you can find God in what they think is greater than man: in nature, in the vast life-force of the universe, or whatever. Christians say, 'No, you are deceived about God; the only image of God is man.' Secularists and humanists believe that, if we are careful, we can be honest and find man by looking at ourselves. Christians say 'No, you are deceived about man; you will not begin to understand man, or yourself, unless you meet Jesus helpless and humiliated on the cross.'

And the cross for us is not just a memory. It is a word preached. We preach simply Christ crucified. It is a word preached which makes us able to recognize Jesus, to know him when we meet him in the casual random encounters we have with those who suddenly need us. Christians do not propose a course of instruction, to learn about Jesus Christ and thus about God. They do not show their disciples a way and a discipline they are to follow in order to understand. There is no straight and settled road towards God. God in man may be anywhere at any time. He is like a thief at night-time. The coming of the Son of Man is like a lightning bolt; you never know when the revelation is to be offered to you. The preaching of the gospel does not explain God to you. It makes you ready, open, vulnerable to the sudden flashing out of divinity at the most unlikely moment – just at the moment when you are most irritable, most likely to reject the importunate boring grasping person who needs you. The gospel makes us ready for the sudden transfiguration of such moments so that at least we can say with Peter, 'It is good for us to be here' (Matthew 17:4).

Chapter 25

Life After Death

A lot of Christians are uneasy about the idea of life after death. Why? Mainly for two reasons. The first is that if such an afterlife is seen just in terms of rewards or punishments, it looks like a rather infantile way of persuading people to behave well in this life. The second is that it seems very difficult, if not impossible, to envisage life after death. Pictures of hell seem to have been largely projections of vindictive or sadistic fantasies. And pictures of heaven are just unspeakably boring.

But we need to give up on the pictures. The way to make any kind of adult sense of life after death is to try to enter into the mystery of human death. And the central truth we must start from (and never get very far away from) is that we preach Christ crucified. We preach this because it is our gospel, our good news. It is, strangely, good news that Jesus of Nazareth was tortured to death on the cross. But it is good news because we believe that precisely by taking on death, by submitting to death out of loving obedience to the demands of that love he called his 'Father', he took on death and conquered it. In itself, human death is senseless. It is only the cross of Christ that makes ultimate sense of human death, indeed makes even of death a focus of hope. This is because the deepest meaning of the cross is resurrection to eternal life. As St Paul says in his letter to the Corinthians: 'If Christ has not been raised, then our proclamation has been in vain and your faith has been in vain' (1 Corinthians 15:14).

If we take this perspective we shall stop thinking of heaven as 'pie in the sky', and we shall stop trying to imagine an afterlife. For of this we know only two things: that it is ours, and that it is to be our eternal life. The first means that it has to be in some way bodily, for, as St Thomas Aquinas says in his commentary on 1 Corinthians, even if my soul is immortal, 'my soul is not me'. The second means that our life, our eternal life, must be now incomprehensible to us. For concerning eternity we know only what it is not, not what it is; for eternal life is God.

But why should I think that human death is in itself senseless? Why do I think that we need the cross to make sense of it? Isn't death the most natural thing in the world?

Well, I think death is indeed natural to all our fellow animals, but not exactly so in our case. Of course lots of other animals find death shocking and grievous. Anyone who has had anything to do with animals socially knows that they can mourn for their companions taken away by death. But in our grief there is something more. When someone we love dies we feel more than shock and deprivation. We feel outraged, resentful. We feel that a kind of injustice has been done.

When an animal dies it is painful for itself and sometimes for its companions; but it is indeed quite natural. A dog or cat comes to the end of its lifetime as a piece of music comes to its end and completion. Even if it dies prematurely by accident, its end is natural and explicable in the larger scheme of nature. But this is not quite true of us. And this, I think, is because we do not just have a lifetime fitting into the rhythms of nature. Rather, we each have a life-story. And that is something more mysterious. Every human life is not just a cycle but an un-finished story which we have been telling.

We have a life-story because by our own decisions we make something of the life we have received. Any cat is indeed the unique individual that every cat is. But that is because of what it has received from nature: its genetic make-up and the various things that have happened to it during its lifetime. But we are unique individuals in a more profound sense. For building upon what we have inherited from our ancestors, and from the tradition in which we have been brought up, we have each made for ourselves, for better or worse, the personality we now have. In this sense we belong uniquely to ourselves.

I oversimplify here, of course. We make our decisions with the help of, and under the influence of, many other people. But they are still our decisions and not simply 'what happens to us'. We are, at least in part, responsible for who we are. So when another animal dies at the hands of nature, nature is simply taking back what she has lent. But when we die at the hands of nature, nature is a usurer taking away more than we received from her. Hence our sense of injustice and outrage. That is why part of our grief and mourning is anger, justified anger at the unfairness of it all. In some way (and it has to do with our life being lived out in language and thought and narrative) we are not just parts of the natural order. We do not just belong to the natural world. We reach beyond it. This is what first of all makes human life mysterious and human death a mystery. And this is why human death is something that needs to be made sense of.

St Paul says that it was through sin that human death came into the world (Romans 5:12). He seems to mean that we can make some kind of sense of human death by seeing it as a penalty. It is not a very reassuring or comforting sense. But at least it gives human death a meaning: we are condemned criminals, condemned to death, which, therefore, fits into some intelligible pattern – into a story, indeed. I have said that we see death as outrageous because through our decisions, through personally enacting our life-story, we have made more of ourselves than the life we have on loan from nature. But maybe instead we have made less. Suppose our making of ourselves were really an unmaking. Suppose we have used our freedom not to intensify but to diminish our humanity (i.e. to sin). Then it is we who have made a dismal sense of our destruction in death. We, and not nature, are guilty of our own deaths. Our lives have been a prolonged suicide.

Yet Paul does not just view death in these purely human terms. He looks at it in the context of God's love for us. He also has an eye on God's plan that we should not just be freely and fully human by our own decisions, (and therefore unworthy of death). For Paul, a crucial fact to be reckoned with is that we are worthy of eternal life, the life which is God himself, because of God's gift of grace. That, says Paul, is God's plan. But our world has rejected this gift of God. We were born into, and live in, a world that, in its basic human structures, has rejected and rejects God's gift and pursues its own substitutes of domination and exploitation – a crucifying world. So our sin is not just a going astray from humanity, but a spurning of God's love. This rejection of God's gift has twisted even our humanity, so that we are bent upon becoming worthy of death. Under these conditions of sin, our death becomes the culmination of the unmeaning of our lives. Death has not only taken from us the meaning of our life in society, with our friends and enemies. More fundamentally, we have thrown away the meaning of life with and in God. We have thrown ourselves on the rubbish-tip of unmeaning. Death for us is damnation.

Well, it is either damnation or the cross. For the good news is that there was one death which was not a sign of ultimate destruction. There was one man whose death was the culmination of a life of loving obedience to God, obedience to the mission he knew he had been given, the mission of being human, really human, with no thought of dominating and controlling others but simply of giving himself away to them: the mission of being wholly vulnerable to them. It was therefore, of course, a mission that, given what we have made of our world, was bound to culminate in being killed by us.

Here was the first human death that was not a symptom of sin but a sign of loving obedience: a sacrament of response to God's love. And the answer of God was to pour out renewed life upon Jesus, to pour out the Holy Spirit in such abundance that the Spirit not merely raised Jesus from the dead but poured out through the risen Christ upon the rest of humankind. Because of this, if, by faith, we are 'in Christ', our death too can be the culmination of our loving obedience. Our death too can be a conquest of death in resurrection.

But Christians do not just grieve for their dead and go beyond their grief in rejoicing that their death is a union with Christ's death and so with his resurrection. They also pray for their dead because they are our friends; for our tradition has yet more to say about death than this. We do not just rejoice with the dead in their union with Christ's resurrection. We are also in solidarity with them in what may be a difficult and painful transition. They have to lose themselves in Christ in order to be really themselves; and this is not an easy thing.

Whenever we sin we not only turn away from God's love; we also turn towards ourselves, get more wrapped up in ourselves. The major evil here, the turning away from God is, paradoxically, the easiest thing to deal with; for God is so besottedly in love with us that we have only to ask for forgiveness to find him eager to restore us to his friendship. The other part, our obsession with ourselves and our own will is not so easy. For sin is a health-hazard. We build up an addiction to our self-flattering illusions about ourselves, a habit that is hard to kick. We can work at it; and that is what penitential practices (designed to make us realistic and humble) are for. All sin involves a kind of self-indulgence; and growing out of this infantile condition, groping towards reality, is a painful business. It involves a kind of practicing for death (we sometimes call it 'mortification', 'making ourselves dead'). Most Christians have recognized that people generally die with unfinished business in this respect (not in getting rid of sin, but in abandoning the humourless self-importance in which sin has left us). We have some growing-up to do, some self-abandoning, before we can be sufficiently our real selves to be ready for our resurrection into glory.

And in this matter we can help each other. For Christianity is all about coming to God in and through our friendship with each other. When those we love have died we can still be with them and help them with our prayers. This is what purgatory is about. We pray for the dead in purgatory not because we doubt that they are being brought to share in Christ's risen life but to help them in their painful process of being stripped, not of sin and guilt, but of the hangover of sin, of their illusions and addictions.

It is as useless to try to envisage or imagine purgatory as it is to envisage heaven. But we ought not to be speculating about an afterlife. What we know is that we have been buried with Christ 'by baptism into death, so that, just as Christ was raised from the dead by the glory of the Father, so we too might walk in newness of life' (Romans 6:4). And we know that 'if we have been united with him in a death like his, we will certainly be united with him in a resurrection like his (Romans 6:5).

Chapter 26

Priesthood

As the book of Exodus tells it, when the people of God were formed out of liberated slaves from Egypt, Aaron and his sons were made the first priests of the new community. Like all the peoples around them, the Hebrews took it for granted that a real established society needed a priesthood – just as we take it for granted that a society needs some kind of Civil Service, or some kind of school system. Aaron was the first high-priest of the children of Israel. He had a job, an important job, within that community. The priest's job was to arrange the transactions with the gods of the community, to ensure that the gods did not become hostile, for this could be disastrous for the people. The priest had to find out what the gods wanted, and he had to arrange for the people to give it to them. So he stood as mediator, on the frontier, looking both ways: to the gods and to the people. And he communicated to the people the messages of the gods, just as he communicated to the gods the offerings of the people.

But, of course, the children of Israel were no ordinary society. They were something unique in human history. They made a gradual but huge revolution from which all subsequent humankind has benefited and (as with all revolutions) suffered too. For by the time the Book of Exodus was put together it was becoming clear that their God was not one (or more) of the gods. And this was going to make a difference to what such things as priesthood meant. The children of Israel were a people who were not to have *any* gods; they were to deal only with one who says 'The whole earth is mine' and 'You shall be for me a priestly kingdom and a holy nation' (Exodus 19:5–6). The only one they can call 'God' (and they are very reluctant to call him anything at all), is not the national god of Israel but the maker and owner of the whole earth. Most peoples, of course, had some story about the god who made the whole world; but the gods they actually worshipped and spent money on were the more immediate ones who were needed for keeping the crops growing and the soldiers successful. Israel was to do without this assistance and to worship only the God of the universe.

So already in the book of Exodus you have the idea that Israel does not just contain a number of priests, like the other nations round about, but that as a whole nation she *is* priest of the God of the universe. Like any priest she mediates between God and the people, but, in the case of this priestly nation, the god is the God of all the world, and the people are the people of all the world. Israel as a whole community is priest for humankind, communicating to *us* about the commands of God, bringing *to God* our prayers and offerings of praise and thanksgiving.

Of course it took some time for all this to sink in; its full implications were not, I suppose, recognized until after the return of the Jews from exile. But in, for example, the later poems in the book of Isaiah it is explicit. Here we find it said that the God the Israelites worship is the creator of all that is, and that in his plan the Jews are to be the priest mediating between this creator and his human creations.

This was his plan for the Jews, and in the fulfilment of that plan something strange happened. Just as the notion of priest had moved from the individual priests (Aaron and his successors), to the communal priesthood of the nation as a whole, so, when the plan came to fulfilment, the reverse happened. It turned out that the priesthood of the Jews was preparing for, and culminated in, one man: Jesus of Nazareth.

He was himself the fulfilment of the hope of Israel. He himself was the point towards which the history of the people of God had been moving. In him the Jewish revolution came to a head. In him was the union of the God of the universe and humankind. As the Letter to the Hebrews tells it, then the last vestige of any national priesthood, the priesthood of Aaron, has become finally irrelevant; not for nothing has the Temple been destroyed. A momentous change has taken place (cf. Hebrews 4:14–15:10).

There was then, almost immediately, a tragic schism in the people of God: between those who saw the momentous change as primarily the destruction of the Temple, and those who saw it primarily as the death and resurrection of Jesus. And until that first and worst schism between what we now call Jews and Christians is somehow healed, neither of us will be whole. But, in the meantime, neither Jews nor Christians have a priesthood. The Jews, indeed, have rabbis to interpret the Law; but they are not priests. We Christians have supervisors and elders (that is what our words 'bishop' and 'priest' originally meant); but they are not priests in the sense that either Aaron or the whole people of Israel were priests. For us Christians, the only priest in that sense is the one who was priest in the fullest and final sense: Jesus of Nazareth. He is the one mediator between God and humankind. He is the only priest as he is the only king, as his sacrifice is the only sacrifice. All priesthood, kingship and sacrifice for the God of the universe have found their real meaning only in this man. And what an extraordinary and paradoxical thing this is. The shocking thing that Christians are saying is that everything meant by priesthood, kingship and sacrifice was nothing religious at all, nothing liturgical or ceremonial. It was all really about the execution of a falsely convicted criminal, an ordinary squalid miscarriage of justice.

We Christians say that, when we look for kingship, judgement and power, we see only the one who is judged and punished. If we look for the sacrificing priest, we see only the victim who is bleeding to death and hanging from a cross. If we look for the sacrifice, we see only a judicial murder. If we look for mystical union with the creator of the universe, we see only the dying victim of our world, the representative of all victims (including the victims of kings and priests). This individual man is our only priest. Yet, in meditating on the meaning of this, the early Christians made a new kind of move from individual back to the whole community again. For they saw the whole community of believers as sharing in the priestly mission of Christ. We find St Peter's first epistle re-echoing and giving new meaning to the words of Exodus ('You shall be for me a priestly kingdom and a holy nation'). But now we are 'a holy priesthood, to offer spiritual sacrifices acceptable to God *through Jesus Christ*' (1 Peter 2:5). Once more, like our fathers, the children of Israel, we are, as a community, priests for the whole of humankind before the God of the universe – to bring God to the world and the world to God.

This is the priesthood to which we are dedicated by our baptism. You might say we are condemned to it by our baptism; for baptism is a kind of sentence of death. The people of Israel, hearing that they were a royal priesthood, may have had fancies of conquering the world for God, bringing it into submission to the creator; but we know that our priesthood is that of Christ; it is the priesthood of the cross; we exercise it only in sharing the passion and death of Christ. And we add nothing to that priestly act of death. We simply share in it. And we share in it as we are in solidarity with all the victims of this world represented by our dying Lord, as we share in *their* suffering and death. This is our first and fundamental priesthood which we all share by baptism. And it is because of this priesthood of all the people of God that those who exercise special and essential ministry for the whole people of God (our overseers and elders, our bishops and priests) have their priesthood. They have a ministry of teaching and leadership in the priestly people which is dramatized by their preaching and presiding at the eucharist. But what they are expressing and exercising in all this is the priesthood which belongs to us all. The ordained priest presides at the eucharist, but what he exercises is the priesthood of us all (the priesthood of Christ). At Mass we *all* consecrate the bread and wine through the ministry of the priest. He is there to represent our priesthood. And, in doing so, he does not just represent the congregation present with him. He represents the baptismal priesthood of the whole Church throughout the world. The presiding priest is consecrated by the whole Church to represent the whole Church; he is there because we are not simply a local group of Christians praying. We are the whole Church praying. So we are Christ praying, Christ offering his sacrifice, Christ handing himself over to us in the form of food and drink, Christ providing the sacrificial meal in which we show our solidarity with each other and with all the victims of this world: the sacrificial meal in which we are in solidarity with the victim on the cross through whom all humankind is brought through death and out of death to unity in the eternal life of love.

Chapter 27

Christian Unity

What does it mean to pray for Christian unity? This is really quite a hard question to answer. If we ask ourselves what Christian unity is or would be, we find ourselves entering deeper and deeper into a mystery. For to seek the unity of Christians is to seek to be united in one Spirit. In the end, the unity of Christians goes beyond what can be expressed by agreement in the words of doctrine. It goes beyond even our shared sacramental life. It has to do with the vision and enjoyment of God himself. As we seek unity amongst ourselves, we are seeking the unity of the Trinity: for this Jesus prayed to his Father 'that they may be one, as we are one, I in them and you in me, that they may be completely one' (John 17:22–3). The unity that is not simply a matter of negotiations and reformulations, but is the gift of God, is the gift of God's own self. It is the unity of the Kingdom. And it is not to be given in full before the Kingdom.

In the meantime, what we really have to be concerned with is not so much Christian unity as Christian disunity. And here we have another kind of difficulty. If we ask what, in the end, Christian unity is about, we find ourselves confronted and surrounded by mystery. If we ask what Christian disunity is, we find ourselves confronted by complexity. There are just so many different kinds of disunity, so many different ways in which Christians have discovered they are separated from each other.

All that the ecumenical movement can do is to seek out and analyse those nearest to hand, and those that seem most likely to be curable, and to try to heal them. We cannot have any grandiose plan for bringing about the unity of all Christians. That would be like having a plan for the total and complete health of all the human race. All we can hope to do is cure some of the wounds and diseases that are close to us.

Notice that the disunity we come across is not the same as diversity. Nor is it the same as sin. But it is connected with both. Then again, Christian divisions do not arise from weakness, from people failing in commitment to Christ. They arise from people striving to be faithful to the gospel while being so concerned with their own kind of striving that they become blind to the strivings of others. Christians *discover*, to their surprise, that they are separated. They wake up one morning to find that it has happened. It is certainly not something they seek. It comes from a kind of neglect of community.

As St Paul tells us in 1 Corinthians, diversity is something necessary and healthy in the Church: 'God arranged the members in the body, each one of them, as he chose. If all were a single member, where would the body be? As it is, there are many members, yet one body. The eye cannot say to the hand, "I have no need of you," nor again the head to the feet, "I have no need of you"' (1 Corinthians 12:18–21). Paul here is thinking first of all of different functions in the Church; but he is surely also talking about different factions, followers of Apollos, or Cephas, or whoever – for the Corinthians were plainly a quarrelsome lot.

There are, and there have to be, many different ways of expressing the gospel, the good news that transcends any possible account of it. There are, and there have to be, different theologies – as there is, for example, a theology of St Luke, and another of St John, which grew up in different churches. Different churches, too, can and should develop different customs, diverse forms of worship. And all these contribute to the one body, to the diversity, the catholicity of the Church.

Division happens in the Church when good people discover that they have been so intensely concerned with their own theology, their own interpretation of the gospel, that they have lost sight of the unity of the body. Or, as is much more common, they discover that *others* have lost sight of that unity. Diversity in the Church is an excellent and necessary thing. But, like many excellent and necessary things, it presents dangers too. It can give rise to a separateness – to the point where Christians feel that others have drifted away from communion, have excommunicated themselves, have preferred their own way to the whole body.

When this happens some churches try to abolish diversity altogether. And others become complaisant about separateness. Hence the monolithic, exclusive, and most uncatholic character of the Catholic Church in the last few centuries. Hence, too, the strange multiplicity of Protestant churches. The answer does not lie either in imposing uniformity or in accepting division. And, unless we find the answer, we move from diversity, which is good, through division, which is not good. We move, in fact, to sin. At this point, the disunity of the Church becomes the sin of the Church. The real sin of disunity does not lie in what has happened in the past. It lies in what is *not* happening in the present: in our failure to heal the divisions. It is not that our fathers have sinned and we, in our superior charity, must do their repenting for them. On the contrary, our fathers were, for the most part, very good men, passionately concerned for the purity of the gospel. But they were limited, as human beings are. And maybe they were a little careless at first. They were taken unawares by the disasters and divisions that followed. What we have to repent of is not the sins of our fathers but our own failure to deal with the mess. The sin of the Church is not the divisions of the past, but the failures of the present. It is the perpetuation of divisions of, say, the sixteenth century – divisions which, though springing from important arguments of great and good people intensely concerned for the truth of the gospel, are now only quarrels of little, mean people concerned mostly for the status of their own groups.

There are real and important arguments for the Church of today which are not at all the same as the arguments of the sixteenth century. Today there are great and good Christians who find they must disagree about, say, the meaning of the Church of the poor – about what it means to preach good news to the poor, to proclaim liberation to captives and to those who are oppressed (cf. Isaiah 61:1–2). So in thinking about Christian unity we need not just a determination to heal the wounds of the past but a warning about new wounds in the future. We need to be warned lest the real disagreements of good people should lead, not by malice, but by folly and recklessness, to new division, to another denial of the one Spirit in which we were baptized.

If we are to face that task of maintaining the unity of the Church now and in the future, we must clear up the irrelevant divisions of the past. And we do that not by forgetting them or ignoring them, but by going back to the Reformation, not simply to repeat the old disputes but to recapture in charity the passion for the truth of the gospel that people then had on both sides. For this passion can take us now not into division again, but toward the one Father, through the Son, in the Holy Spirit of love.